# Making A Superintelligence

## AI safety and the Control Problem

Utkarsh Verma

To future me,
I hope you still have a job.
And if you don't, I hope the problems in this book
are solved by then.

# Contents

Preface      i

Chapter 1. Timeline of AI      1

Chapter 2. The AI takeover      20

Chapter 3. The AI      56

Chapter 4. Goals      71

Chapter 5. Reasonability      88

Chapter 6. Side effects      110

Chapter 7. Mesa-optimizers      137

Chapter 8. Oversight      148

Chapter 9. Uncertainty      162

Chapter 10. Deception      174

Chapter 11. Philosophy      191

Resources of change      225

References      231

# Preface

*"If we use, to achieve our purposes, a mechanical agency with whose operation we cannot interfere effectively... we had better be quite sure that the purpose put into the machine is the purpose which we really desire."*

~Norbert Wiener, 1960

Humans are intelligent. So intelligent in fact, that we refer to other animals that are significantly less intelligent than us to compare our own intelligence amongst ourselves. Our intelligence is magnificent. It is unprecedented, unrivalled and unorthodox in how much more superior it is to everything else we encounter.

Chimpanzees share about 99% of their DNA with humans[1]. This means that there exists a 1% divergence in DNA which has caused every one of the differences between the two primate species. Some of this divergence comes from physical differences, humans do not possess as much hair and typically have a less pronounced brow ridge than chimpanzees. Another subset of this divergence comes from behavioural differences, chimpanzees remained on all fours while we adopted bipedalism. These changes were incredibly useful for the survival of early humans, but they were in no way extraordinary enough to make us any different from the other animals of the time.

However, a small portion of this DNA divergence comes from a difference in our brains. The environment was such that our predecessors were rewarded for being more intelligent. They could identify which berries were safe better, they could trick animals into traps. Those humans who possessed marginally greater cognitive abilities had a marginally higher likelihood of producing offspring. About a million years ago, this animal with a marginal cognitive advantage discovered fire. Another five hundred thousand years later, they created stone-tipped spears. Twelve thousand years ago, they started farming and created civilisations. Now, this marginal cognitive advantage is the reason why we completely and utterly dominate functionally every single ecosystem on the globe.

This less than 1% difference is the reason why you can read this book. Somewhere inside your cranium lies an organ, your brain, that can process these strange symbols and shapes into meaning. A diverse group possessing this organ has created the intricate and complex society we live in now. A society which deals with objects, concepts and plans that are so incredibly out of the grasp of a chimpanzees' understanding. It would be fruitless for the chimpanzee to even begin to comprehend the daily life of a human, forget standing up to the intelligence of any human authority.

Now, consider if one day this intelligence is challenged. If one day we create a superintelligent machine that has an even greater general intelligence than us, then our advantage would become obsolete. This machine may dominate over our society, possibly to the same extent or even greater than how we dominate over chimpanzees. It would have every capacity to assert absolute control on us. This machine would be our last invention. Considering that today all four of the chimpanzee subspecies are endangered, it would be in our interest that we keep this machine under our control.

We are now at a time where there is a very real possibility that this machine may be created, potentially during our own lifetimes. Artificial General Intelligence (AGI) refers to a hypothetical form of artificial intelligence that possesses the ability to understand, learn, and apply knowledge across a broad range of tasks and domains, similar to the highest level of human intelligence. AGI has remained the long standing goal of AI research, however its viability has only recently actually begun to be taken seriously. In the late 1990s, a startup called Webmind, led by AI researcher Ben Goertzel, aimed to create a digital baby brain that would become fully self-aware and surpass human intelligence. Goertzel envisioned a transition equal in magnitude to the advent of intelligence or the emergence of language. These goals however were deemed delusory and overly zealous, and the company went bankrupt shortly later. Now there are very real and very serious companies and researchers convinced that AGI can be built within the next few decades[2]. This means that we face the problem of control very soon as well.

This book discusses the possibility of AI superintelligence and some problems that will arise because of it. It is very possible that this challenge will be the most daunting one humanity has ever faced. It is also very possible that we may fail this challenge before even knowing we were supposed to do something about it. Hence, this book serves to introduce the problem to a greater population of people (besides the crazy-haired researchers on niche forums that make up the majority of discussion today) to inspire greater interest into these problems.

A large part of the issues brought up incur a technological problem, but many require to be viewed from a philosophical lens as well. It is for this reason I highly recommend you explore these topics with an interest for both. Though, admittedly, if you had asked me about my interests in philosophy before really doing the research for this book, it would have been next to none. However, I have gained an interest in the subject from the research I did for this book. I thus recommend those who are in a similar situation as I was before to be open to philosophical thinking through the medium of the problems as well.

Many of the points made in this book may be wrong. It is very plausible that this book will be irrelevant in 10 years or so. I have tried to the best of my ability to extend this period of relevancy for as long as possible, yet it is almost inevitable that there are some considerations of critical importance that are missing which are undoubtedly necessary. Hence, this book is not supposed to be taken as objective fact, but rather as a general guideline for greater research. Unlike most writers, I dearly hope that this book becomes irrelevant as quickly as possible, as it means that we have made meaningful progress into these problems.

# 1.

# Timeline of AI

## History of AI

After the end of the second world war, there was a growing number of scientists who started to gain an interest in the thinking capabilities of machines. At the time, machines were beginning to hold a significant population in production lines and people were now coming to accept their presence in society. Machines gradually increased in complexity and abilities. The term "artificial intelligence" was first coined in 1955 by John McCarthy, an American computer scientist. The very next year, a group of scientists gathered at Dartmouth college to discuss how these machines can be made to "learn". This is seen by most as the birthplace of AI, though Alan Turing had previously already paved a path in exploring the abilities of machines through mathematical proofs of the possibility of creating these machines and through physical demonstrations of their abilities in deciphering German communications.

This group was determined to test the limits of these machines. They applied for funding from the Rockefeller Foundation, writing the following;

*"We propose that a 2 month, 10 man study of artificial intelligence be carried out during the summer of 1956 at Dartmouth College in Hanover, New Hampshire. The study is to proceed on the basis of the conjecture that every aspect of learning or any other feature of intelligence can in principle be so precisely described that a machine can be made to simulate it. An attempt will be made to find how to make machines use language, form abstractions and concepts, solve kinds of problems now reserved for humans, and improve themselves. We think that a significant advance can be made in one or more of these problems if a carefully selected group of scientists work on it together for a summer."* [1]

The Dartmouth Ten, as they were called, worked with tools which were, by todays measures, childrens toys. Revolutionary Multi-million dollar computers of the time such as the IBM 7030 or the IBM 305 RAMAC are surpassed by the modern Raspberry Pi 4. Still, the group remained optimistic, and managed to craft machines which could solve "intelligence" problems that people did not believe any machine should be able to do. For example, the General Problem Solver (GPS) of 1957 was able to solve a broad range of problems by representing them in a problem-space framework. The Perceptron attempted to model the human brain's way of thinking and learning from experience with regards to image recognition, laying the groundwork for neural networks. They even created "Shakey the Robot" later in 1966, which was a mobile robot capable of perceiving its environment and making decisions based on its perception autonomously. It showcased one of the first integrations of sensory input, planning, and output in the form of action.

Nine years after Dartmouth, researchers started to envision the future that such AI research may entail. Irving J. Good, who was on Turing's team of code-breakers at Bletchley Park, started to question what the end goal of such research may look like. Good wrote,

"If mankind builds a machine that can surpass all the intellectual activities of any man, and since the design of machines is one of these intellectual activities; there would then unquestionably be an "intelligence explosion", and the intelligence of man would be left far behind. Thus the ultraintelligent machine is the last invention that man need ever make, provided that the machine is docile enough to tell us how to keep it under control"

Thus, the idea of the Singularity was born; a point in time where humanity loses all control of progress to its own creations.

However, this initial optimism in the '50s and '60s did not last. In the decades that followed, AI research came to a halt, not by a bang, but by a whimper. The research never stopped because of some grand revelation which prevented us from progressing, but merely lost funding as the field began to seem overhyped. Researchers also were reaching the limits of the computing power they had at their disposal. The potential of the field had yet to be reached.

In the 1980s, there was a resurgence of interest in expert systems, computer programs designed to emulate the decision-making abilities of human experts. These systems used rule-based reasoning and knowledge representation to solve specific problems. Prominent examples include MYCIN, an expert system for diagnosing bacterial infections, and Dendral, which analysed mass spectrometry data for organic compound identification. These systems, however, required extensive training data which could only be achieved through manual input. Their ability to adapt into new and uncertain environments was limited as well, making their use cases extremely limited. At the same time, neural networks gained attention as well. Algorithms such as backpropagation and Recurrent Neural Networks (RNNs) were developed, laying the foundation for modern AI systems. Still, researchers were heavily limited due to computational power.

By the 1990s, AIs started to reach the point where they were beginning to be better than the best humans at, tasks, specifically board games, that humans prided themselves into believing no AI could ever beat them. In 1994, a programme called Chinook took the World Checkers/Draughts Championship after defeating the then-reigning world champion, Marion Tinsley. The programme Logistello beat the world Othello champion, Takeshi Murakami, 6-0. And, in perhaps the most famous human defeat at the hands of AI, the programme Deep Blue defeated the World Chess Champion Garry Kasparov in a six-game match in the same year. Suddenly, AI was winning. The public finally were made aware of these systems. They were increasingly interested, and afraid, in the capabilities of AI systems.

*Fig 1.1: Kasparov playing against Deep Blue, 11th May 1997*

Nowadays, losing to an AI at a board game may seem somewhat childish and insignificant. But, you must realise, most people believed that these games were too complex for a machine to understand them. Chess was the game of human intelligence. Beating the best chess players was an attack on human intelligence itself. "If one could devise a successful chess machine, one would seem to have penetrated to the core of human intellectual endeavour" [2] It was unfathomable at the time that these mere machines could possibly stand a chance without essentially recreating human intelligence itself.

In fact, these feelings toward board games lasted far into the 2010s with games such as Go, until AlphaGo beat Lee Sedo 4-1 on March 15, 2016 (Highly recommend the documentary on it [3]). AlphaGo was different, in that unlike its predecessors in chess, it was never taught to play; rather, it was taught to learn. It was not a chess or checkers or Go algorithm, it was a learning algorithm, which taught itself how to play and practised against itself millions of times. AlphaGo Zero, the successor of AlphaGo, grew significantly stronger than the original algorithm without ever seeing a real game of Go. Right after its achievements in Go, AlphaZero used the exact same algorithm to learn chess, achieving superhuman performance with mere hours of training.

In the past 2 decades, AI has indiscriminately began changing every industry. It has become difficult to name one where AI has not been implemented in one way or another. People have gotten accustomed to using AI systems in the background of practically every activity. AI has begun to find new cures to diseases, started optimising supply chains, and has been investing billions of dollars every second on the stock market. AI has a better understanding of the medicine and drugs you take than your doctor. It checks your credit cards for suspicious activity. It has helped me find and fix a countless number of grammar and spelling errors in this book already. Try to name an industry that has completely sidestepped the use of AI. If you tried to google it, you just used AI too. Everywhere you look, the consensus is clear. AI Is the New Electricity[4].

Very recently, AI has left the hands of industrial professions. It has instead begun everyday use by everyday people. Real, tangible models such as Large Language Models (LLMs) and image generators are now available to the public, and their usefulness is undeniable. With tools such as DALL-E, ChatGPT and the dozens of voice replication software, AI has become unavoidable in the current modern world. Now, any random person can, to varying degrees of effectiveness, do the work of entire teams of people from just their desktop.

The things AI is as good at or better than humans are now broader than ever. The next logical question is, when will AI achieve *general* intelligence? When will AI be truly better than humans at every intellectual problem we can solve?

# Predictions of AI

So, you want to know when AI will replace you. The logical course of action would be to try and ask some experts. These people have a better understanding of these machines than almost anyone on the planet. Surely, these people, with years of experience and research will be able to give a somewhat cohesive answer. A study[1] in 2015 did just that, it asked 352 experts who had published in the 2015 NIPS and ICML conferences when AI will achieve "High-level machine intelligence", or when unaided machines can accomplish every task better and more cheaply than human workers. So, they conducted the survey, consolidated all the results and came to the conclusion:

Nobody has any idea.

There was a massive variation in each researcher's answer. Some predicted us to have HLMI by 2025, while others said we will never achieve HLMI at all. Asian respondents expect HLMI in 30 years, whereas respondents from North American expect it in about 74 years. On average, the aggregate forecast predicted a 50% chance of HLMI occurring by 2041 years, and a 10% chance of it occurring within 2025 years. Still, the majority of respondents would have heavily disagreed.

To further undermine any persons ability to predict AI development, a subset of the researchers were asked a slightly different question: "When will all occupations be fully automatable?" That is, when for any occupation, machines could be built to carry out the task better and more cheaply than human workers.

Logically speaking, this question is very similar to the first question. If an AI could achieve HLMI, they would be able to automate any human job. It was only a minor change of wording between the two questions. It hence would be reasonable to expect that the two should occur at the very most a decade or so apart from each other. However, this simple tweak changed the results drastically. The aggregate predictions were significantly farther into the future compared to the first question. Respondents on average predicted that there was a 50% probability that all human occupations could be automated by 2138, and a 10% probability by 2036.

On top of all this, the study asked the experts when AI will reach certain "milestones" when they would be capable of completing a task with human-level performance. For example, experts predicted that machines would be able to beat all Atari games by 2024, or that AI will be able to write a Highschool essay by 2026, and would be writing best-selling books by 2049. One of these milestones was Go. The aggregate prediction was by 2028, some of the more optimistic researchers predicted it to be by 2020 or so. AlphaGo beat Lee Sedo in the same year which experts predicted that it would take AI another 12 years to reach human-level play. (The predictions also measured that the most difficult job for AI to replace would be: AI research.)

Perhaps more concerningly than all of this is how the predictions have changed since. The most recent variation of this study in 2023[2] showed that there had been an overall significant fall in how long AI experts predicted it would take for important milestones to occur. Some milestones were pushed back, for example the average predicted date for a machine to beat all atari games got pushed to 2029. However, the vast majority of them were predicted to be much closer than before. The predicted time for AI to achieve full automation of human labour fell by 30 years, and the time until the automation of specific jobs such as surgeons and AI researchers fell accordingly. This only further gives evidence for how uncertain we are about the future of AI.

*Fig 1.2: 2022 and 2023 Aggregate forecasts*

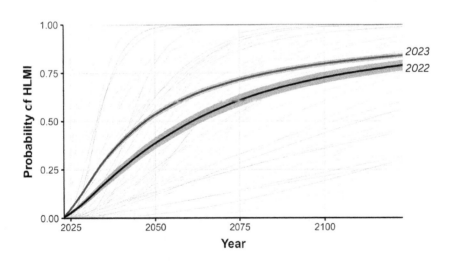

The only thing researchers agree on is that they disagree on everything. But why is this the case? Well, as Eliezer Yudkowsky puts it, there is no fire alarm for Artificial General Intelligence[3].

In an experiment in 1968, eight groups of three students were asked to fill out a questionnaire. Soon after, the room they were in started to fill with smoke. Five out of the eight groups did not respond to the presence of the smoke, even as it became dense enough to make them start coughing. Later experiments show that individual students would respond 75% of the time, while a student placed in the same room with two actors who would not respond themselves, would only respond to the smoke 10% of the time. These experiments as well as others show the phenomenon of pluralistic ignorance. The students did not want to seem too panicked and overreact, so they waited for a response from the other students, who were also trying to do the same.

A fire alarm on the other hand provides a distinct instruction, that there is a fire and that everyone needs to evacuate. "A fire alarm creates common knowledge, in the you-know-I-know sense, that there is a fire; after which it is socially safe to react." as Yudkowsky puts it.
A fire alarm is not any better as an indicator of fire. In fact, it is much more likely that there is a fire if there is smoke than if there is a fire alarm. A fire alarm is false 98% of the time[4], but smoke is almost indisputable evidence of a fire. Rather, a fire-alarm gives up the heads-up that we should act. When the students

hesitated while responding to the smoke, their main worry was not about the fire or how they should evacuate to safety, they were worried about what the other students may think of them. "The reluctance to act is the reluctance to be seen looking foolish, not the reluctance to waste effort."

With AGI, there will be no fire alarm. There might be smoke: a breakthrough or two which impresses the world. In fact, we might be in that smoke already. But, there will be no clear indication of when we should act. No large company will announce that they are x years away from building an AGI, likely even they would not be certain that it is possible until it is built. Most experts think that we are quite a few years away from creating an AGI. But at the same time, most experts also thought we were over a decade away from a machine beating humans at Go when AlphaGo beat Lee Sedo.

AI scientist David McAllester writes how when he asked John McCarthy, a pioneer of the field, when he believed HLMI would be achieved, he said *"between five and five hundred years from now"*. According to McAllister, *"McCarthy was a smart man"*[5]. Yudkowsky also mentions on a podcast in 2011, *"I would be quite surprised to hear that a hundred years later AI had still not been invented, and indeed I would be a bit surprised ... to hear that AI had still not been invented 50 years from now"* [6]

Nevertheless, many researchers have tried to use various methods to give a data-backed estimated date to when we will achieve Artificial General Intelligence (such as expert opinion[1], economic modelling techniques[7] and the Kurzweil's Law[8]). As a general consensus, most of these papers estimate it to be around mid-century, between 2040s to 2060s. This is a very short timeline, this is a future either we or our children will live to experience. Still, it seems quite a ways away. Surely we are able to deal with this problem in the following 20 years or so, why should we care about this problem now?

# Why You Should Care

Whenever high-level AI safety is discussed, there are a few common responses that tend to come up. The problems of AI safety seem simple at first. It is thus that many fall easily for the Dunning-kruger effect.

Fig 1.3: *The Dunning-Kruger graph*

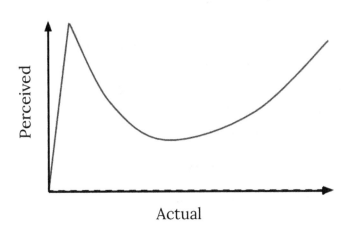

The cause of these responses is often due to a lack of imagination for what superintelligent machines could look like, which stems from incorrect assumptions about what they would be. These refuse to be tenable under further investigation and analysis.

Most people's first interaction with the idea of a superintelligent machine is through media. These interpretations of superintelligent machines do somewhat address problems that we may face with an actual AGI machine; Ultron came about as a villain in the Avengers universe because of the misalignment problem. However, the finer details of these interpretations forgo realism in favour of a little cinematic flair. It is unlikely that AGI would create thousands of punchable humanoid machines and try to use a whole city as an asteroid. It is because of these misinterpretations that many people develop stereotypical behaviour that they assume is true for all superintelligent machines.

I found the most effective way of cleaning out these assumptions is by quickly rebutting some initial responses that you possibly may have. This is borrowed from a paper by Stuart Russell[1] and from a talk he gave at the Future of Life Institute[2].

## "We will never develop true AGI"

The end goal of AI research has always been to eventually develop a program capable of human-level intelligence. As development has ramped up at an increasing pace, most researchers predict that we can develop an AGI by 2040, with some even suggesting that it may be possible to develop one by 2028. The thing is, there is no evidence supporting the idea that there exists a physical limit which prevents us from achieving general intelligence. Nature has already achieved this long ago; humans are proof that AGI can be achieved biologically. There is yet to be a reason why it cannot also be achieved artificially. As of our current knowledge, there is nothing that our meaty brains can do that our computer chips can't, including achieve general intelligence. Moreover, this statement essentially is betting against human ingenuity. This would not have been our first time doing so either. Many times in the past, people have claimed that some technologies were impossible right up until someone had a revolutionary idea that made it happen. For example, the Nobel prize winning scientist Ernest Rutherford once said in a famous quote;

*"Anyone who expects a source of power from the transformation of these atoms is talking moonshine."*

This quote was published in the Times on September 11, 1933. Just 16 hours after being published, Leo Szilard went on a walk and thought of a method of creating a self-sustaining nuclear reaction. Dismissing the possibility of developing a true AGI is irresponsible and has potentially disastrous consequences if we continue without care.

## *"It is too early to worry about it now"*

The time when we should start worrying about a problem depends on not only when that problem occurs, but how long we need to overcome it as well. The issue with this sentiment is that we will likely not know when it is the right time to take action. The solution to AI safety is a technologically complex one, but it also likely involves our society undergoing some philosophical and ethical changes as well. If indeed the solution lies in a philosophical shift in our society, we likely will not find a solution any time soon. On top of this, we do not actually know how long we have before this issue arises. As mentioned before The first AGI could be closer to us than we think. We do not know when we will build the first AGI. As mentioned before, the time it took for a revolutionary idea to form that defied the beliefs of established and highly regarded scientists was less than a day. The first AGI can be 20 years away, or be developed over the coming weekend. It is impossible to accurately predict beforehand when such a technology could be developed.

## *"It's like worrying about overpopulation on Mars when we have not even set foot on the planet yet"*

A variation of the previous sentiment, this analogy comes from Andrew Ng[3]. It is convenient for two reasons: the risk is far in the future, and it is also seemingly very unlikely that we will ever have this problem in the future at all. However, the truth is that we are already developing very capable AI systems. Moreover, a problem like overpopulation of Mars is easily telegraphed by the number of people on the planet, and can be easily forecasted through estimated birth rates. We have no means currently of getting an accurate prediction of when we would ever build AGI, or even any AI system intelligent enough to be dangerous, and have even less means to handle one properly. A more apt analogy would be a plan to move the human race to Mars with no consideration for what we might breathe, drink, or eat once we arrive.

## *"Just put it in a box"*

As a piece of software, it is true that it is theoretically possible to restrict an AGI completely to a completely independent from the external environment. However, this is unrealistic for two reasons.

For one, if the superintelligent AI ever has a reason to escape, it is very likely to overcome any barriers we place for it quite easily. It is impossible for humans to build a superintelligence-proof method of confinement. As we will discuss in chapter 8, restricting a superintelligent AI is forming an adversarial relationship between us and it. Any adversarial relationship with superintelligence is an uphill battle, except the hill is more like a cliff.

Secondly, for an agent to be useful, it must have an impact on the world. Say we do manage to build a magical box that guarantees the superintelligent AI will not be able to escape. Since it cannot carry out plans on its own, its only purpose would be to act as a question answering machine. Lets say you give it some task, such as to improve nuclear energy, and it returns you some intricate plan that involves many parts and steps you do not understand. How do you verifiably prove that this plan would be safe? It is very possible that this plan would be too complex for any human to comprehend.

Given the possibility remains that this superintelligent machine could be misaligned, would you still enact this plan? How do you ensure that this plan would not sabotage the confinement of the AGI, or allow the AGI to create sub-agents that carry out its misaligned goals for it?

Eliezer yudkowsky hypothesizes how a superintelligent machine could theoretically use the influence we already give computers today.

*"My lower-bound model of "how a sufficiently powerful intelligence would kill everyone, if it didn't want to not do that" is that it gets access to the Internet, emails some DNA sequences to any of the many many online firms that will take a DNA sequence in the email and ship you back proteins, and bribes/persuades some human who has no idea they're dealing with an AGI to mix proteins in a beaker, which then form a first-stage nanofactory which can build the actual nanomachinery. The nanomachinery builds diamondoid bacteria, that replicate with solar power and atmospheric CHON, maybe aggregate into some miniature rockets or jets so they can ride the jetstream to spread across the Earth's atmosphere, get into human bloodstreams and hide, strike on a timer.*

*A cognitive system with sufficiently high cognitive powers, given any medium-bandwidth channel of causal influence, will not find it difficult to bootstrap to overpowering capabilities independent of human infrastructure."*

# 2.

# The AI Takeover

## What it will look like

It is surprisingly difficult to define superintelligence. We all have a general idea of what a superintelligent being would be. For something to qualify as superintelligent, it must at the very least be exceedingly better than the best humans at a given task. This sounds about right. Though, by this definition, a calculator can also be said to have superintelligence as well; a human with a good calculator significantly outperforms any human at high-level mathematics questions.

Instead, a better definition for a machine which is "superintelligent" is that it must outperform the best human intelligence at a wide range of cognitive tasks. It must have general intelligence. In modern instances, there are various types of examination-style tests used to pit humans against AI systems[123], some designed specifically for AI testing while others are taken from general human tests. As of writing, these AI models have succeeded in achieving high level intelligence comparable to the best humans at certain tasks, and in many forms have gained the ability to surpass human intelligence to some capacity at specific tasks. Yet, they have been unsuccessful in ultimately surpassing peak human general intelligence.

Consequently, we would also need a definition for intelligence as well. Most dictionaries define it somewhat similarly to that of the Oxford dictionary;

**intelligence**
*noun*
/ɪnˈtelɪdʒəns/
[uncountable]

1. the ability to learn, understand and think in a logical way about things; the ability to do this well

While this provides a pretty decent framework, this isn't really a quantifiable metric. We need something to compare and differentiate more intelligent agents from less intelligent ones, and this definition does not allow us to do that very well. We are unable to assess the internal cognitive structure of an agent, at least not to any degree of accuracy, to determine if it is actually learning and understanding. (Also, this definition opens up the debate of whether machines possess the capability to "understand" at all, which is a whole other topic we will leave for chapter 8.) Hence, for the purposes of this book, we can define intelligence as the effectiveness of decision making towards a goal. This may be a little vague for some scenarios. Nevertheless it allows us, to an extent, to make an objective ranking of the intelligence of agents for any given goal. Eating a salad is a more effective decision compared to eating a cupcake if your goal is to lose weight. Hence, eating a salad is the more intelligent decision. A greater intelligence is capable of making a more effective decision compared to a lesser intelligence. This directly allows us to directly link the actions of an agent with its intelligence, as an agent which is more intelligent will take actions that perform better towards a given goal.

As mentioned at the start of the book, humans are immensely intelligent agents. We each possess countless abilities across a wide range of tasks. We have complex thoughts and ideas, we have deep rooted cultures and religions. We are also completely replicable. We know that evolutionary processes are capable of, within some billions of years, producing a general intelligence; us. These evolutionary processes were completely blind in nature, in that they were completely random and improved only through natural selection over a multitude of generations. Hence, it is very likely that a similar process but instead guided by a human programmer should be able to do at least the same, if not more. And if this process can undergo generations of improvement within a relative blink of time, we should be able to create an intelligent being in much a shorter period of time as well. This observation has been used by some philosophers and scientists, such as David Chalmers and Hans Moravec[5], to argue that human-level AI is not merely theoretically possible but feasible within this century.

Using this logic, it should be theoretically possible to replicate the natural processes until we replicate human intelligence. Of course, this would be an unfathomably large task. Multicellular life has existed for 600 million years[6]. According to estimations by Nick bostrom in his book Superintelligence: Paths, Dangers, Strategies, if we were to simulate 1025 neurons over a billion years of evolution, and we allow our computers to run for one year, these figures would give us a requirement in the range of $10^{31}$–$10^{44}$ FLOPS. The most powerful computer now would be the The Frontier system at the Oak Ridge National Laboratory (ORNL) which is capable of running one exaFLOP per second, or $10^{18}$ FLOPS. If we wanted to complete this task, we would need to convert every kilogram of the earth into a supercomputer of the same capabilities as the entire Frontier system.

This plan is highly inefficient in terms its usage of computational resources. We could significantly reduce the number of these calculations by a number of orders of magnitudes by taking shortcuts. Not every evolutionary change results in an increase in intelligence. Many evolutionary changes may even be harmful in maximising intelligence, such as when accounting for the evolutionary costs of maintaining the energy requirements of such an intelligence. It is difficult to estimate to what extent these calculations can be cut; it could be by an order of magnitude of five, ten or twenty. The feasibility of replicating the development of general intelligence through natural processes would be determined by the importance of the degree of resolution in facilitating the simulation.

These calculations should also be taken with a grain of salt, as it is possible that we are just being a victim survivorship bias. It is difficult to estimate how likely it really is to create an intelligent being because we only have one example to work off of; ourselves. We can draw parallels of estimating how much we would need to simulate to produce intelligent life to finding intelligent life in our own universe. It is possible that we will face the same problems in simulating evolution of intelligence as nature has faced in producing intelligence in the universe. The Fermi paradox is the discrepancy between the apparent high likelihood of the existence of advanced extraterrestrial life and the lack of conclusive evidence of it. According to physicist Enrico Fermi's estimation of the likelihood of intelligent life sprouting on a planet, there should be many signs of detectable alien life. However, we have yet to discover any. There is hence reason to believe that there are factors which have not been considered which determine how likely it is for intelligent life to come about. In reality, the creation of intelligent life is probably also heavily dependent on luck. It may be that for every 10^30 planets that seemingly could support intelligent life, that only one ends up being able to produce it. Thus, if we were to run our simulations, we may find that we would have to run it a further 10^30 times before we can successfully produce human-level intelligence, which would be a significant blowback to how much computational power we would need and would make the completion of the task in human timescales impossible.

Another possible method of replicating human intelligence would be to replicate the brain itself. The brain may be a perfect template from which we are able to build a digital intelligence. We would not even need to create a perfect adult brain. Alan Turing proposed as early as back in 1950 that we could build a "child-machine" that initially starts as a simple machine and raise it to become superintelligent.

*"Instead of trying to produce a programme to simulate the adult mind, why not rather try to produce one which simulates the child's? If this were then subjected to an appropriate course of education one would obtain the adult brain."*[7]

However, we can expect this technology to be generally far from what is currently possible. There are various technological advancements that would need to happen before we can reasonably start to hope to emulate the human brain. The sheer complexity of the human mind means that it will require a large amount of technological ability, resources and time before we can attempt to do so. Hence, it is reasonable to assume that we would have some sort of heads-up before anything of that sort would happen, and the chances of such a technology surprising us is low. We should have ample time to prepare if such technology becomes a reality.

The method of achieving superintelligence we will be focusing on this book is AI. To achieve general intelligence, we can create an AI model in one domain and training it with detailed datasets such that it achieves intelligence in other domains as well. For an AI to learn in other domains however, it must have some incentive to gain intelligence within these fields which will bring it closer to completing its goal. Something like a chess AI has little interest with anything not related to chess. It would not perform any better at chess if it understood quantum physics and bioengineering, so training it on more chess games will not push it to achieve intelligence in any other domains.

A text prediction model however does have a use for these things; if the preceding text has any mention of these topics, then it would be useful to understand these topics to predict what words would come next. It is for this reason that models such as GPT-4 have demonstrated such a wide range of intelligence in many different domains. For instance, it has shown a fairly decent ability to solve questions in mathematics[8], entirely as a root of its main goal of predicting text. It is this ability for language to hold importance in so many domains that holds the interest of companies such as OpenAI with the goal of creating AGI.

There are some that hold the belief that the efficacy of such a method will slowly depreciate as the improvement observed in singular-domain models levels off. However, this is only an assumption, and from a technical standpoint holds no real bearing. GPT has remained closely aligned with the prediction in improvement using scaling[9] and multi-modal models such as GPT-4 have seemed to exceed the scaling laws that governed them. This is the reason for the optimistic consensus of the capabilities such models can achieve through just improvements in scale.

All these methods present the possibility of eventually achieving at minimum a level of intelligence as good as that of humans. It is for this reason that we must be aware of what the final product of these methods may look like. The largest variation in how these AI-systems turn out to be comes from the level of intelligence we achieve. Near-human intelligence will result in a model that has a cognitive capacity similar to what we are already with, along with features that make it very different all at the same time. On the other hand, a system possessing intelligence significantly greater than humans poses a much less predictable and understandable model. This consequently makes it a much larger problem for AI safety. Depending on which we end up creating, our current level of preparedness varies greatly.

## Near human intelligence

It may be possible that we will be unable to go much beyond human intelligence. The greatest intelligence we have observed is that of humans. It may be that the best human intelligence is close to some maximum intelligence already. This would explain why whales and t-rex's do not exhibit superintelligence even though they possessed larger brains with more neurons and hence much larger raw cognitive computational power. There may exist a limit for intelligence, beyond which we cannot exceed. If such a limit exists, and given we are very close to it already, then the best AI systems would also be limited to an intelligence close to that of a human. Another possibility could be that we may face technological problems during development that themselves require superintelligence to overcome. This would essentially make us unable to achieve superintelligent AI, as we would be unable to overcome these challenges ourselves. Hence, this would hinder us from building anything significantly more intelligent than us.

We know that it should be, in principle, possible to at minimum demonstrate a general human-level intelligence digitally. Hence, we can reasonably assume that one day we will likely build a machine capable of intellectual thought, decision making and long-term planning at the level of the best humans. Such a machine would be able to complete any intellectual human task as good as the best humans. It would not be limited by discipline or differences in skill requirements, which already makes it more powerful than any single human at basically anything.

The machine would also receive the benefits of being a machine. Humans are pretty bad at a lot of cognitive problems because of the fact that evolution had not optimised for such things. For example, humans can't do mental arithmetic very well (What is 17×87?). Some humans are significantly better than others, but even still, we lose out quite badly compared to our machine counterparts (Its 1,497). Our superintelligent machine would not be limited by this. Even if it is bad at doing mental arithmetic itself, it would probably simply run a calculator programme to do the calculation for it. Same thing if it had to play a game of chess, the machine intellectually might be only be as good as a human, but it could also run its own chess programme instead. Hence, the machine would be as good at a task as the best humans or as good as a computer, whichever is better.

If we are able to replicate human-level intelligence in a machine, we can also assume that this machine would be able to run at an exceptionally larger speed. This assumption stems from the assumption that general intelligence is parallelizable. Parallelizability refers to the idea that we can divide a task or process into smaller, independent subtasks that can be executed simultaneously. We can run a parallelizable system twice as fast if we have twice the hardware capabilities. Most modern high-level AI systems use ML frameworks such as Tensorflow or some other alternative, all of which are parallelizable. Hence, it is reasonable to assume that we should be able to run an AGI faster using better hardware.

Intelligence can be defined as the effectiveness of decision making. An agent which possesses greater intelligence can formulate better decisions which result in greater performance. However, this definition omits an important factor which can affect the effectiveness of an agent's decision making: time. Agents are able to make more effective decisions by taking more time to formulate them. It is for this reason that the overall effectiveness of decisions generally increases over time. A student will most likely perform better on a test when given 30 minutes instead of 5 minutes. The students cognitive abilities had not changed at all, however the extra time to make decisions would allow the student to appear "more intelligent".

The extent of this increase however reduces over time, as the marginal improvements that can be made from spending more time on a decision falls. After an infinite amount of time, we can observe that an agent will settle on a decision of finite effectiveness. We can hence use this asymptote of effectiveness to determine an agents true intelligence. I.e., the intelligence of an agent is defined as the *final* decision it makes.

We can graph the general trend in the effectiveness of decision making of an agent over time as the following:

Fig 2.1: *Effectiveness over time*

However, using the final decision of an agent to represent its intelligence is unrealistic. Most, if not all, decisions made have at least some kind of limit to the amount of time that can be spent. And even if the agent is not explicitly limited by time, it must at the very least eventually come to a conclusive decision such that the decision can be carried out. It is for this reason that the true maximum potential effectiveness cannot be reached.

When comparing the intelligence of two agents, we usually take the effectiveness of the decisions made after a reasonable time interval. This usually results in the more intelligent agent making better decisions after the time interval.

*The AI Takeover*

For example, between the two agents, the more intelligent one will come to a more effective decision at $t_1$.

Fig 2.1: Difference in true intelligence

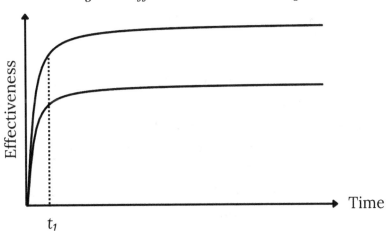

However, this is not necessarily the case all the time. For example, one agent of equal final intelligence to another can still be perceived to be widely more intelligent by formulating better decisions faster than the other one.

Fig 2.2: Faster intelligence

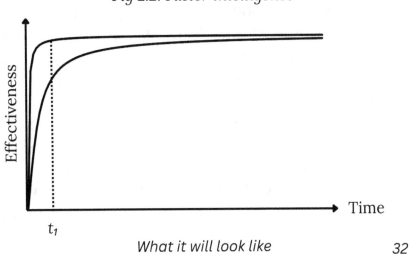

Even though the two agents are technically equivalent in terms of final intelligence, one appears to be more intelligent than the other at $t_1$. This would also translate to it be more useful in regular scenarios as well, and hence would be strongly preferred over the other agent in real life problems.

It is for this reason that an artificial intelligence equally as intelligent as humans would potentially still be able to be significantly more "intelligent" than us. This is because we would be able to run AGI much faster than humans, such that the effectiveness of decisions made by AGI systems would be far greater than those made by humans in an equal amount of time.

This form of intelligence is known as a speed-superintelligence, because of its ability to do everything the best human intelligence can do but a lot faster. By "a lot", it would likely be in the order of a few magnitudes in terms of time to complete tasks. If you could run your brain at 1000x its current speed, you could think about your actions for 1000x as long. When you speak to someone, you could think about what to say, the different ways the person would react to what you said, whether your words could have any unintended implications or meanings, how what you said would affect the person in the future. You would seem much more intelligent, even though your actual brain is all the same. An AGI developed on electrical hardware would be able to be limited to the speed of electrical impulses, which travel at the speed of light. The speed of light is over a million times faster than the speed of neural transmissions. If bounded only by the laws of physics, an AI is only really limited by this. Such a machine would be vastly superior to a human brain in every way, even if it is just as intelligent. A machine capable of processing human-level intelligence a million times faster can complete a PhD thesis within a handful of minutes, or a decade's worth of work within about 5 hours. As the name suggests, speed-superintelligence would be quite quick.

Such a machine would be not limited in its Input-output (I/O) speed either. Us humans are limited to a pair of eyes that can only see one screen at a time. Our fingers can only type at about 40 words per minute. We communicate through vocal languages at around a measly 40 bits of information per second[10]. We only have 5 senses: sight, hearing, touch, smell, taste, of which the last 3 don't come in very handy when it comes to handling vast swaths of data. We rely on graphs and pie charts to translate this information into something meaningful to us. Our meaty, hunter-gatherer bodies come in the way of efficiency in a multitude of ways. Our speed-superintelligence would not have these drawbacks. It would have the capacity for much greater I/O speeds, only limited by the mechanical hardware it has access to which can also improved. It wouldn't need to see or hear data either, it would be simply able to experience it altogether, reducing the time it takes to process information to be nearly instantaneous.

A machine reading this piece of text would experience it as a whole, it wouldn't rely on visual stimuli or need words to be in a nice orderly left-to-right line. It would decode the message immediately, regardless uʍop ǝpısdn ǝɹǝʍ ʇı ɟı or यह हिन्दी में हो.

A speed-superintelligence would appear to be significantly more intelligent in regular scenarios to humans, simply because it has more relative time to make its decisions. As a consequence, a speed-superintelligence would see us as unbearably slow. A superintelligence capable of thinking a million times faster would experience time moving a million times slower as well. This time dilation would make human-speed frustratingly slow. To it, the human reaction time would take multiple days. It would hear us complain about Mondays for thousands of years each week. Such a being might choose to only converse with other sped up minds rather than bother talking to our species. It may only choose to preside in its digital world instead of the material one, simply because the material world is too slow for its liking.

And, as if these advantages were not enough, it would have a couple of extra perks as well. For example, even if the AI is heavily limited by hardware capabilities equal to that of the brain, it still would be able to use this hardware much more efficiently. When you are thinking about something, some people choose to close their eyes, or prefer to work in a quiet room. This might minimise the data being inputted into their brain. What they can't do is completely reform the brain structure into using all of its computational resources on a problem. You can't convert your visual cortex to help you do arithmetic, our brains simply do not work that way. An Ai would make much more efficient use of these resources. AI is also replicable between different machines. Humans have painfully slow methods of conveying information. Students spend years in school before learning calculus. An AI however can simply copy and paste a calculus AI's internal structure into another machine, without having to do weekend homework or pesky group projects.

Still, this superintelligence would be constrained to the laws of physics. At such intellectual speeds, the speed of light becomes an increasingly large problem. Any and all communication would take an excruciatingly long time. Communication with another superintelligent machine on the other side of the planet would take several hours. Speaking in this manner would be about equivalent to you having to take a plane back and forth to deliver each message. This might mean that these systems may choose to congregate at one location to minimise the long-range communication.

However, we can deduce that this system's rate of improvement will be manageable in the long-term. This near-human level intelligence machine would be reliant on large swaths of data. To continue improving its own performance and abilities, it would need to accumulate increasingly greater amounts of data and hardware.

Hence, the rate at which this machine can get better should slow down as it becomes better. Every unit of optimization power, the amount of quality-weighted design effort, put into improving the machine would have diminishing returns in intelligence.

Fig 2.3: *Marginal improvement*

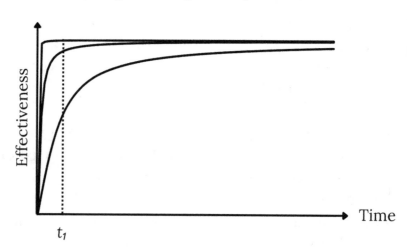

*The AI Takeover*

## Post human intelligence

So, we know that human-level artificial general intelligence should be possible. However, there is nothing theoretically preventing AI from exceeding this. In fact, if we were to look at the wider picture of how other species compare to us, we should even expect AI to exponentially improve in intelligence beyond what our measly human minds can even begin to think. Yudkowsky describes how what we describe as intelligent and stupid is vastly disproportionate to the real scale of intelligence.

*"For us humans, it seems that the scale of intelligence runs from "village idiot" at the bottom to "Einstein" at the top. Yet the distance from "village idiot" to "Einstein" is tiny, in the space of brain designs. Einstein and the village idiot both have a prefrontal cortex, a hippocampus, a cerebellum.*

*Maybe Einstein has some minor genetic differences from the village idiot, engine tweaks. But the brain-design-distance between Einstein and the village idiot is nothing remotely like the brain-design-distance between the village idiot and a chimpanzee. A chimp couldn't tell the difference between Einstein and the village idiot, and our descendants may not see much of a difference either."*[11]

With almost anything that has gotten automated, computers have gone from not being able to do something to doing it way better than humans. There exists very few fields where a computer can do something humans can, but much slower and less efficiently. If general intelligence were to follow this trend, it could be capable of recursively improving itself at a pace unmatchable by humans. Such an AI may be capable of an intelligence explosion, a singularity.

Singularities are a fancy way for researchers and scientists to say "We have no idea what will happen now". It is the point of no return, when the machine's intelligence would be beyond our control. What such a superintelligence would look like is unknown. However, we can still attempt to prepare for such a possibility.

We will only be able to attempt to thoroughly explore beyond-human intelligence after a machine achieves it. Only then can we truly prepare and develop methods of handling such intelligent beings beyond the speculation we currently do. This poses the question: how long will it take for us to go from manageable human-level intelligence to radical superintelligence?

# The transition

Given that AI will eventually become more intelligent than biological brains, and that the capabilities of such a system would far exceed its human counterpart, it can be said that all parts of human technological development can be at least to an extent supplemented with AI. This would also include the development of AI.

Assuming that development of increasingly more powerful AI systems will continue, AI will progress to a point where it will aid in its own improvement. This would essentially create a feedback loop, where intelligent AI systems will create even more intelligent AI. Eventually, it is likely that AI will be vastly responsible for its own development and improvement and contribute to a majority of any developments made. At this point, humans will no longer have control over how and at what pace AI is developed, and will neither have control over the direction which AI development takes. From here, the machine's intellectual capabilities would be independent from humans, and it will improve largely or completely on its own. We can call this point the singularity, where humans no longer are required in AI. After this transition into the singularity, humans would functionally have lost control, it would serve as a point of no return. So, given that it will eventually surpass human intelligence, how long will it be from then until a machine reaches a point of independence in its own improvement?

There are 3 general time scales in which we could transition to a singularity, as highlighted by Bostrom in his book[1]: Slow, Moderate or Fast. Which occurs would depend on the pace of improvement of the AI when transitioning between human-level intelligence and an independently self-improving superintelligence. Note that this is different from the question asked in chapter 2 to the experts. Previously, we discussed how long it would be from now till human-level intelligence. On the other hand, the speed of transition relies on how long it would be between human-level intelligence and independent improvement. AI may take a long time to reach human-level intelligence, yet transition to radical super-intelligence quickly, and vice versa.

*Fig 2.4: The transition*

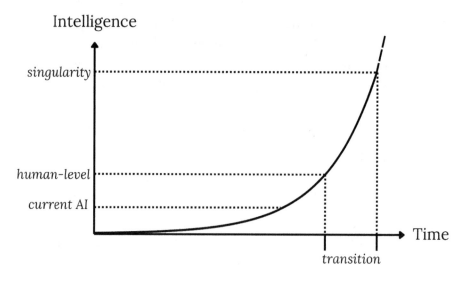

*The AI Takeover*

A slow transition would occur over a long temporal period, somewhere between multiple decades or centuries. A slow transition would allow us ample time to adapt properly to the existence of intelligences as good as or greater than our own. We would be able to develop new political systems around its existence. We can train new experts to research it and its inner workings to a greater degree. We will be able to properly account for people of certain groups who may be unfairly affected by them. New systems and infrastructure can be developed to deal with it safely. We would be able to inform the public adequately about any new innovations or developments regarding superintelligence. Nations could properly negotiate international treaties regarding the weaponization of superintelligence. In such a case, we will be much more prepared for the onset of superintelligence, that we stand the best chance to deal with it.

A moderate transition would be one that lasts over months or years. This would give humans some time to develop a response to the new developments, however it would not be enough to make major reforms to current systems to account for it. We would likely have time to distribute information regarding any developments to important figures; company heads, government officials, trusted experts. However, it is possible that information may only be released between relevant influential people, and kept secret from the public as the events unfold. Humans may be able to create some protocols and infrastructure, but we would likely not be able to thoroughly test their viability or effectiveness. They will likely be built by panicking governments and haphazardly picked groups of individuals. There would be large-scale changes to the world's economic, political and social systems. Moderate transitions would offer chaos, from which there would be winners and losers. Some groups of individuals may find themselves a unique opportunity amongst the upheaval to benefit enormously, resulting in great inequality and imbalance of power.

Lastly, a fast transition would be one that spans over mere days, hours or minutes. A fast transition would allow humans next to no time to react. It is likely that we would not even realise that it had occurred until after it is too late. Humans would have lost the fight before it even began. Even the most steadfast and in-the-know leaders would find it basically impossible to deploy a response at all. In a fast transition, humanities fate would be completely reliant on preparations made prior to the transition. If the preparations are insufficient, all humans would be at risk equally, regardless of power or influence.

It may appear to some that a slow transition is more likely to happen compared to a moderate or fast one. This would place the transition more closely aligned with other large eras of humanity which brought widespread change to our daily lives, such as the agricultural (multiple millennia) industrial (decades to centuries) and the information revolution (~50 years).

The internet already brought such widespread change at an unprecedented pace that it is unfathomable that anything could ever radically change our lives any faster. It seems implausible that humanities dominance over intelligence can be overruled within just a couple hours.

However, there is reason to believe that a slow transition is improbable. Rather, the transition would likely be an explosive one. To understand why, we would need to understand the factors that would affect such a transition. The speed of improvement of the system would be dependent on two variables: the amount of optimization power put in and the responsiveness of the system to improvement. Bostrom coins the inverse of this responsiveness "recalcitrance". Hence, we can define the rate of change of relative intelligence, $I$, of the systems over time as the optimization power, $P$, put in over recalcitrance, $r$, of the system.

$$\frac{dI}{dt} = \frac{P}{r}$$

While it is difficult to quantify the intelligence of a system, the optimization power or the recalcitrance, we can still observe that the speed of transition would be dependent on the amount of effort applied and the efficiency of converting that effort into intelligence in the system. The transition would happen faster either if there is a large effort put into improving the system (high $P$) or if minor efforts resulted in massive improvements to the systems intelligence (low $r$).

Both the optimization power and the recalcitrance of the system is not constant. They would be affected by various external factors. Hence, we can conclude that the speed of transition would be dependent on these external factors and how they change the rate of change of the AI's intelligence.

Let's take a look at recalcitrance first. We can change the initial equation into the following to better understand how recalcitrance has changed.

$$r = \frac{P}{\left(\frac{dI}{dt}\right)}$$

It may appear to some based on gut-feeling that as AI improves from human-level intelligence to the singularity, recalcitrance will increase. This would make logical sense, as it seems likely that at greater levels of intelligence, achieving a marginal increase in intelligence will require increasingly greater amounts of optimization power.

However, in some situations, it is possible for recalcitrance to be low. For example, if AGI is only one key insight away from being achieved, then any improvement beyond general human-level intelligence can be achieved very quickly. When this final obstacle is overcome, AI may jump from a very rudimentary intelligence to a very high intelligence quickly. If this is the reality of current AI, then we should expect recalcitrance to be low.

In another scenario, it is possible that recalcitrance be low due to the fact that the models capabilities are handled by two different subsystems, a domain-specific decision making system and a generalised decision making system. For instance, a model may be trained on a wide variety of data but specialise with information pertaining to nuclear physics. In this case, the model may have domain-specific techniques which excels at nuclear physics related problems and a general-purpose reasoning ability which handles other problems. It could be that while the generalised subsystem is below a certain capacity threshold, it contributes little or nothing to the overall performance of the model. However, if a small amount of optimization power is invested such that the generalised subsystem overcomes this threshold, the improvement in performance may vastly increase, as the generalised subsystem can pull from a large variety of fields to piece together information about nuclear physics, beyond which the domain-specifics could achieve alone. For this reason, it would appear that the improvement of the intelligence of the overall model is very high with relatively low optimization power being invested, hence resulting in recalcitrance being low.

It is also possible that our anthropocentric view of intelligence may lead us to overestimate recalcitrance when thinking about beyond human-level intelligence. Recall Yudkowsky's argument that the difference between intelligent humans and stupid humans is very low compared to overall intelligence of things. For this reason, it could be that we also overestimate changes in intelligence beyond human-level intelligence. Hence, the normal growth of intelligence in AI systems may appear to be very high. The difference in intelligence between human-level intelligence and the singularity may be similar to the difference between Einstein and a village idiot; high with respect to humans but low when considering the intelligence of all things in our universe.

The other factor in our equation of the speed of the transition is optimization power. When a reinforcement learningagent is given training data, it can use this data to further optimise the optimizers such that future results are better. We can call the amount of optimization that the RL agent can conduct its optimization power, P. For any given task in a particular environment, a certain amount of optimization power is needed to find a policy that works well. We can define the minimum bits of optimization power needed to find this policy as the number of times we must split the space of all the possible policies until the remaining subset of policies perform at or above the minimum acceptable performance, i.e. the performance lower bound.

What we are left with are a certain number of bits of information which define the location of the polices which excel at or beyond the performance lower bound in the greater space of all possible policies. The optimization power is the number of bits necessary to define these policies.

As mentioned previously, the transition would involve a period where AI technology represents a large, but not yet majority, of its own development. Essentially, intelligent AI will be used to create even more intelligent AI. We can say that the optimization power that can be applied by an AI is proportional to its intelligence. Assuming that recalcitrance remains equal and the system's only source of optimization power comes from itself, we can write that:

$$\frac{dI}{dt} = \frac{cI}{r}$$

We can solve this to get the exponential function:

$$I = Ae^{\frac{c}{r}t}$$

This suggests that even if recalcitrance remains constant, the rate of improvement would be exponential.

This is not to be taken as conclusive evidence that a fast transition *will* happen. It is rather difficult to predict how particularly more advanced technology would evolve into the future, especially with regards to how difficult it would be to make software improvements to a human-level AI. However, a fast transition should be taken as a very possible fate for AI development, and hence we should prepare for it as well.

To some, the fact that a fast transition is a possibility, and that we are currently very equipped to handle it, seems to provide a convincing argument against the development of AGI. If a fast transition is truly the more likely scenario, and given that this scenario involves our AI almost immediately falling out of our control, it seems unwise to continue development towards a point of no return. Given the potential consequences of superintelligence, they may argue that the most intelligent action that we can take currently would be to prevent any further development of AI until we have protocols in place if a fast transition occurs; that we should not further develop AI technology until we are sure we can handle it.

# Yet, we will

With the takeover of AI being such an unknowable and possibly imminent threat, perhaps we should not venture down the path of AI at all. Or at least, this has been a growing consensus between various important figures and the general public. This has led to the creation of a letter[1] from the Future of Life Institute asking for a pause on large-scale AI experimentation. It has been signed by various major players and leaders in technology, such as Elon Musk, Stuart Russell and Steve Wozniak. The letter received large scale news coverage and serves as a stepping stone towards a complete pause on AI development. It hopes to pause high-level AI development until we first develop methods of safely operating these machines and can guarantee that we will benefit from their development.

*"AI systems with human-competitive intelligence can pose profound risks to society and humanity, as shown by extensive research[2] and acknowledged by top AI labs.[3] As stated in the widely-endorsed Asilomar AI Principles, Advanced AI could represent a profound change in the history of life on Earth, and should be planned for and managed with commensurate care and resources. Unfortunately, this level of planning and management is not happening, even though recent months have seen AI labs locked in an out-of-control race to develop and deploy ever more powerful digital minds that no one – not even their creators – can understand, predict, or reliably control.*

Contemporary AI systems are now becoming human-competitive at general tasks, and we must ask ourselves: Should we let machines flood our information channels with propaganda and untruth? Should we automate away all the jobs, including the fulfilling ones? Should we develop nonhuman minds that might eventually outnumber, outsmart, obsolete and replace us? Should we risk loss of control of our civilization? Such decisions must not be delegated to unelected tech leaders. Powerful AI systems should be developed only once we are confident that their effects will be positive and their risks will be manageable. This confidence must be well justified and increase with the magnitude of a system's potential effects. OpenAI's recent statement regarding artificial general intelligence, states that "At some point, it may be important to get independent review before starting to train future systems, and for the most advanced efforts to agree to limit the rate of growth of computers used for creating new models." We agree. That point is now.

Therefore, we call on all AI labs to immediately pause for at least 6 months the training of AI systems more powerful than GPT-4. This pause should be public and verifiable, and include all key actors. If such a pause cannot be enacted quickly, governments should step in and institute a moratorium."

-Future of Life Institute

This decision is almost assuredly the correct thing to do. Rationally speaking, it is dangerous to continue any further development in AI. We have repeatedly been surprised by AI and its capabilities in the past, and it is possible that one of these surprises in the future would have major consequences. It is strongly supported by people with unparalleled knowledge and insight in the industry. And, despite my own plight for caution when designing ever increasingly better AI systems, I believe that such a pause will not happen.

I may come to eat my words, governments have the ability to create policies that facilitate the pause very quickly. Congress can announce these policies next week. And I hope that these governments make me eat my words too. It would be even easier for AI companies to announce that they will refrain from building more intelligent AI systems as well. However, I believe that this will not happen for 3 main reasons.

For one, improving AI technology has generally been good so far. AI technology has seen widespread growth and investment, mostly because of the staggering benefits it can bring. AI technology has been instrumental in the detection of cancer. AI algorithms, trained on vast datasets of medical images, can analyse radiological scans like X-rays, MRIs, and CT scans with remarkable accuracy. This allows them to detect abnormalities or potential signs of diseases that may be challenging for the human eye to discern. It has reduced the occurrence of false positives and false negatives dramatically, aiding us in providing the proper treatment to those who need it most. It has helped create new treatments for Ebola[4] and helped us gain a better understanding of countless diseases.[5] Autonomous cars have reduced the rate of crashes by over 65%, and reduced the rate of crashes with risk of injury by 74%.

Alongside this, as AI develops at an exponential pace, it uncovers new benefits exponentially as well. This makes it difficult to place any one date from which we should pause AI development. We could potentially be missing out on countless benefits and lives saved just by pausing AI development for a handful of months. The letter asks for no further experimentation using AI more advanced than GPT-4. However, GPT-4 alone has brought such extensive benefits across industries, that developing the technology further is tempting. As of writing, Google also has shown interest in developing powerful AI models, with its Google Bard attempting to compete with OpenAI's GPT-4. The potential gain from continuing is just too great for any individual team, company or country to stop.

Furthermore, the benefits of having better AI capabilities than your opponents is as much an economic as it is a military concern. Countries have vested interests in pushing domestic AI firms to build stronger AI tools for use in the military. They remain as a major source of financial investment into AI[7], and this only increases as AI shows more convincing results.

Secondly, we are also not certain about how long such an AI pause should last. The Future of Life Institute states a duration of 6 months. However, we would very likely need a much longer period of time to fully develop the safety measures necessary. In fact, we are unsure of how to even begin to answer many of the questions posed by high-level AI systems, as they stem from philosophical questions scholars have been asking for centuries. There is no clear path that we can follow to build these safety measures. This means that the duration this pause would need to last is not only uncertain, but possibly indefinite.

Lastly, it only takes one team, company or country to create an AI capable of transitioning to independent improvement. This group of people would suddenly have their hands on the most powerful single piece of technology humanity has ever possessed. These groups are selfishly incentivised to build these powerful AI systems, because doing so would likely mean an unreachable level of power over your competition. As mentioned in the previous chapter, the transition is likely to be a fast one. This means that being just months behind your competition could mean being completely dominated by them; mere months could mean a difference between the cutting edge and completely obsolete technology. Suddenly, the development of AI is no longer for the betterment of humanity, but rather an arms race. Even if a treaty placing a complete pause on AI development is put into place, those that choose not to follow it will be rewarded greatly.

As it has been shown, it is not possible for humanity to stop the development of potentially dangerous AI through policy alone. The sheer force of competition , alongside the difficulty of determining the transition and yet ease of crossing it, make for a scenario where corporate PR statements and even the law cannot be trusted. Thus, our best course of action would be to progress our research of AI safety faster. This involves tackling the safety problems that remain unsolved. To do so, we must attain a better grasp of how the AGI systems will work.

# 3.

# The AI

## SAM

To understand how AGIs will work, we must first understand Markov's Decision Processes (MDPs). MDPs are a mathematical framework which helps us understand how an agent chooses its actions. They are based on the Markov property, meaning that the future state of the system depends only on the current state and action, not on the sequence of states and actions that preceded it. The property of being independent of any past factors simplifies the analysis of an agent's choices, as the relevant initial properties would always be the same. MDPs are particularly useful for situations where an agent interacts with an environment over a sequence of discrete time steps, making decisions to achieve specific goals. For our examples, we will use the MDPs in the form of SAM.

SAM (which stands for State-Action Machine) is going to be our hypothetical AGI guinea pig. SAM possesses maximum human intelligence and decision-making capabilities in all relevant domains equally. SAM closely resembles that of Bostrom's speed-superintelligence as mentioned in the previous chapter.

SAM is an agent and has a goal, and its goal is to optimise for the maximum reward possible.
At any time, SAM is in an environment of some state, s.

*States (S): States represent the current configuration or situation of the environment. States capture all relevant information needed to make decisions.*

At any point of time during a training episode, SAM can perform an action $a$, which will cause a transition of the current state from s to s'.

*Actions (A): In each state, the agent can choose from a set of possible actions. Actions are the decisions or moves that the agent can take to transition from one state to another.*

*Probability of Transition (P): Transitions represent the probability of changing state. For each state-action pair (s, a), there is a probability distribution $P(s' \mid s, a)$ that defines the probability of transitioning to the state s' when action a is taken in the base state s. Not all actions result in a guaranteed state. If SAM drops a coin, it is guaranteed to fall on the floor, but not guaranteed to land heads. Hence, $P(s^{floor} \mid s, a) = 1$, but $P(s^{heads} \mid s, a) = 0.5$.*

SAM is intelligent. It can choose to take some actions and not take others. It chooses the actions it takes based on the state that it is in and the potential states it is able to transition to. SAM hence follows a policy to determine its actions.

*Policy ($\pi$): A policy is a strategy that specifies the agent's behaviour. It defines a mapping from states to actions, indicating what action to take in each state. SAM follows, tests and amends its own policy until it achieves the optimal policy, $\pi^*$. An policy $\pi^*$ describes a policy that, when followed, maximises the expected cumulative reward over time. Finding the optimal policy is often the primary goal in solving MDPs. A policy can be either deterministic or stochastic.*

SAM can also have a reference of timeframes. When making a decision, It is often necessary to value the decisions' effects with respect to when they will happen. Some actions are more beneficial in the short-term, while others return better rewards in the future. It can decide to choose some actions over others based on their short-term and long-term rewards by calculating the discount factor of that action.

Discount Factor ($\gamma$): The discount factor $\gamma$ determines the importance of future rewards relative to immediate rewards. A higher $\gamma$ places more emphasis on long-term rewards, while a lower $\gamma$ prioritises immediate rewards. $0 \leq \gamma \leq 1$.

Using a certain policy, SAM can determine the policy's value function.

*Value Function (V): The value function V(s) represents the expected cumulative reward that the agent can achieve when starting in state s and following a particular policy π. It quantifies the desirability of being in a particular state.*

Another fact about SAM is that it is a perfectly Bayesian Neural Network(BNN)[23]. Bayesian Neural Networks refer to extending standard networks which can resist overfitting, a situation where the model learns to fit the training data too closely, capturing noise and random fluctuations that are specific to the training data but do not generalise well to unseen data. BNNs get their name from the Bayesian approach[4], which refers to the method of considering all data as a statistical probability such that all data points have a probability distribution attached to it. This includes the model's parameters, such as the value of weights and biases within the architecture of the neural network. They work by taking in data from a source, or "sampling", and using it to update a probabilistic model about the source's outputs. This helps prevent overfitting in scenarios of scarce data and produces better results for a vast number of tasks. SAM is a "perfectly" Bayesian Neural Network as it fully adheres to Bayesian principles and methodologies.

A drawback of BNNs is that they are difficult to scale to larger problems. However, we assume that this is not a problem for SAM, and that SAM can implement the Bayesian principles without any hindrance from issues in scaling.

In a sense, SAM can be seen as the most intelligent agent whose actions we can reasonably predict. Its intelligence is just enough to imitate all humans, but not much more than that. While we still are hopeless in challenging its intelligence alone, we should still expect its actions to not be radically different from what we imagine it to take. It hence makes the perfect Guinea pig when it comes to dealing with AI safety problems, in hopes of expanding our solutions developed with SAM to the possibly even more intelligent agents of the future.

# Reward functions

In many of the problems we visit, we will use the concept of reward to define a goal for SAM to pursue. Reward functions (sometimes known as utility functions) serve as a method of converting real world data into a quantitative value which is meant to represent the performance of the system in regards to a task. In essence, the reward function, $R$ takes in a world state, $s$, compares it to the base state, $s_0$, and outputs a reward, $R(s_0, s)$. This reward is calculated using the differences between the two states, and it is meant to evaluate the progress made through this transition of state with reference to the goal of the agent.

Many of the problems we discuss later depend on the principles of SAM acting based reward function. This begs the question: Why have a reward system at all? A large portion of the misalignment problems we will discuss results in extreme and inhuman actions. Hence, it may seem that the root of this problem is the extreme, inhuman reward system. It seems naive to assume so definitely that future AI systems would have any explicit reward function at all. In fact, many AI systems being developed today already are not driven by an explicit reward function, such as evolutionary algorithms which work based on the principles of natural selection or generative adversarial networks (GANS) which adversarially train two models to outperform each other. Future AI systems need not be created using rudimentary reward functions, so why try to use a reward function to predict their decisions at all?

Human "reward functions" also are seemingly more complex and diverse compared to just using a single number. Even if we use some form of reward function, it may be possible to implement a more complex and meaningful one. Instead of an oversimplified, linear reward function which can only either increase or decrease, we could try and implement multiple reward functions that interact with one another to form a multidimensional system of preference which would more accurately represent that of our own.

However, while it is true that AI must not explicitly use a reward function which is linear in nature, all AI systems that we build will function similarly to that of a standard reward function. This is because the reward function is a system of evaluating preference, and preference is a core part of any agent's behaviour and in determining all its actions, including that of AI.

In order for an agent to have a goal, it must have a preference. Given any 2 states of the world, an agent must have a method of deciding one over the other, or choosing that it is indifferent to either one. The method of deduction, its preference, for one state over the other is determined by the agent's very goals. For example, let's say it is my goal to eat some cake. For this reason, given a world state in which I am eating a cake and one which I am not, I will have a preference for the former.

If an agent possesses a defined goal and, consequently, exhibits preferences, it is assumed that these preferences adhere to the principle of transitivity. Transitivity implies that if the agent prefers option A over option B and option B over option C, then it logically follows that the agent prefers option A over option C. This ensures a consistent and coherent ranking of preferences across multiple items, but it also means that we will encounter a clear linear trend of valuing one over the other. This is absolutely necessary if an agent wants to progress a goal; if an agent has a circular preference system, it will be stuck in ever changing state and preferences, which will not allow it to pursue any goal.

The reward function is merely an extension of the system of preference. It places a value on each option, which allows you to quantitatively compare options amongst others and place value to specifics in the agent's environment. For example, I may prefer a large cake to a small one and be indifferent between a large cake and two small ones. From this, given an arbitrary reward for any option, we can deduce the reward for all other options using our system of preference. If we assign a large cake a reward of 10, then a small cake would inherit a reward of 5 and no cake at all would take on a reward of 0.

Hence, regardless of the presence of a specified reward system, the AI will form its own system of assigning different rewards for the different items and environmental states it cares about in order to achieve all the goals it has.

However, this easily evaluable form of comparison does not apply to the real world. Humans have to face decisions between very different items frequently. When doing so, what we observe is that humans often choose inconsistently, that different things are evaluated very differently. Hence, a logical next step would be to create a multidimensional reward system. Specifically, this means placing each item of value on its own axial dimension to better represent the complex environment the agent is in. This would allow us to better compare and analyse inherently different objects between each other, which should better resemble the diverse and complex desires of humans. Let's say we want our AI to consider a healthy variety of fruits, so we have explicit rewards for both apples and oranges. We can represent this as a 2 dimensional space of potential states.

Fig 3.1: Comparing apples to oranges

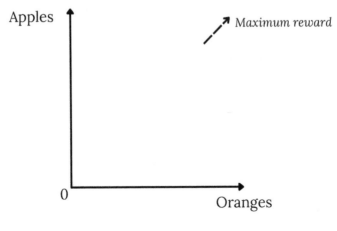

According to the transitive law, there must be some ratio of apples to oranges that have equal preferential value. There must be a ratio at which the apples and oranges have the same value. If no such ratio exists, one of the fruits would have zero value and it would not be considered in the behaviour of the AI. For the cake example, this would be a ratio of 2:1 when comparing the big cake and the small cake. Though, this is applicable to options that are not metrically comparable to each other as well. Let's say that we prefer apples, such that 2 apples is worth 5 oranges. Using this ratio, we can draw a line which connects all the options which provide the same value. For example, if three apples have the same preferential value to SAM as five oranges, we can draw a path crossing all the states which have the same preferential value to six apples, or fifteen oranges. (You may recognise the shape of this graph, if you have taken economics, as a PPC graph.)

Fig 3.2: 2 apples to 5 oranges

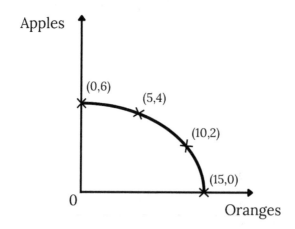

*The AI*

These lines form an arc connecting the two axes. The distance between the base state, that of no oranges or apples, to any point on this arc is proportional to the reward that the agent would receive from transitioning to that state, $R(s_0 , s)$. Hence, the radii of these arcs measure the reward derived from any transition of state. These radii are always a single linear line, regardless of the dimensions of the explicit reward function. Hence, our multidimensional reward system would work identically to a regular linear reward function, trying to maximise the radii of preference to find the most preferential state just as our linear reward function maximises for reward to find the state of greatest reward. The complexity of the agent's true reward function is irrelevant in the decision making process of the agent, as the transitive nature of our preferences results in the linearity of the AI's evaluation of any world state.

If that is the case, why do humans not follow a straightforward policy of maximum reward like an AI? The complexity of human goals is in fact not derived from the complexity of the human reward function (our brain), but derived from the randomness of human preference. Our AI is simply too perfect and consistent at modelling the system of preference. In human decision making however, our preferences are not consistent, they differ between state and time. They are based on subjective views of the environment. Take for example that on a particular day, you no longer want to eat oranges. Eating any more oranges will make you feel

If that is the case, why do humans not follow a straightforward policy of maximum reward like an AI? The complexity of human goals is in fact not derived from the complexity of the human reward function (our brain), but derived from the randomness of human preference. Our AI is simply too perfect and consistent at modelling the system of preference. In human decision making however, our preferences are not consistent, they differ between state and time. They are based on subjective views of the environment. Take for example that on a particular day, you no longer want to eat oranges. Eating any oranges will make you feel sick, and hence eating more does not benefit you at all. For this reason, the entire axis for oranges has a maximum at 0. In such a case, you will simply maximize for the number of apples.

*Fig 3.1: Orange anitpathy*

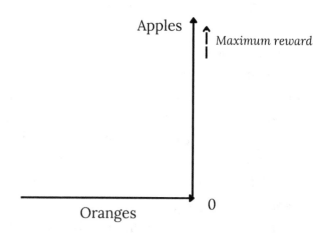

The only way for our agent to have a more human-like understanding of reward is to simply change the reward function to imitate the constantly changing human system of preference. This would mean that the optimal policy would be to replicate the randomness of human preference. The inhumanness does not stem from the reward system, but rather the consistency of the goals of an AI. While the imitation of the human's randomised preference may be desirable in some scenarios, it is in many applications regarded as harmful to effectiveness and potentially even dangerous. We will talk more about human imitation in chapter 5.

Alongside this, reward functions are important as they are effective when the agent is choosing between exploration and exploitation by quantifying the value of each option. At any point of time, the agent can choose from actions using the information it has about its surroundings. It can also choose actions which enhance its knowledge about its surroundings. For example, let's say SAM is in a casino filled with various types of slot machines, and it has the goal of obtaining the maximum possible amount of money possible. Each slot machine has an unknown probability of rewarding SAM an unknown amount of money. Initially, SAM pulls on a slot machine. It on average consistently gives SAM some money. SAM has information about this slot machine and how much it outputs. SAM also knows that there are other slot machines that could possibly output greater rewards. In this case, SAM has 2 options; pull the level of a known slot machine or explore other slot machines.

Exploration tends to have a higher discount value while exploitation tends to have a lower discount value. By choosing to explore, SAM sacrifices its possible short term gains from the known slot machines in exchange for the possibility of finding a more lucrative slot machine, which increases its possible long term gains.

Sparse reward functions tend to increase the agent's willingness to explore. Reward functions which provide rewards less frequently result in agents which receive less information, hence incentivizing them to explore more. This can lead to agents developing more creative solutions to their given tasks. For example, if SAM is never given a reward for turning on the oven, it may try to bake a microwave cake, which may end up being more efficient overall. Sparse reward functions can be useful in revealing solutions that humans may have overlooked. However, an agent's reliance on exploration to discover rewarding actions can slow down the learning process and increase the risk of suboptimal policies.

Reward functions can also be used to explain agent penalties. Penalties the agent to obtain the maximum cumulative reward, by getting as high of a reward with minimum penalty. Penalties help limit the range of possible paths an agent may take to complete the task. Common penalties include penalising distance moved or time taken. These penalties push the agent to use the most efficient and simplest paths possible. Reward functions that heavily penalise negative outcomes or prioritise safety may lead to more conservative, exploitative behaviour. Agents in high-stakes environments, where mistakes carry significant penalties, might prefer exploitation to avoid the risks associated with exploration.

Hence, barring some unforeseeable, radical shift in how an agent thinks, future AI systems will follow clear linear reward functions and optimise for defined policies. This will happen regardless of what its goal may be or whether we give it an explicit reward function to begin with. For these reasons, the regular reward system is very likely going to be a necessary and unavoidable part of the decision making framework of any future AI, and considering its presence is necessary in AI safety research.

# 4.

# Goals

## Instrumental convergence

AI systems are agents, and by definition have goals. An agent's actions are dictated by their goals. For this reason, understanding the goals of an AI is important in ensuring they take safe actions. It may seem easy to understand and correct these goals due the programmable, artificial nature of these machines. Agents we encounter in our regular lives - such as humans, corporations, or governments - tend to have complex goals which we cannot directly influence. On the other hand, most AI systems act based on whatever their reward function is set to, which is much easier to comprehend and change to our desires. However, the problem arises when there exist goals beyond the ones we set. This is the idea of Terminal and Instrumental goals.

Terminal goals are goals that agents follow without reason. These goals are the final objective for the agent. For the sake of simplicity (and at the risk of entering a philosophy debate), let's say that the human terminal goal is to maximise happiness. To do so, we take actions to further this goal. We take actions like eating ramen, celebrating birthdays or going skydiving because these actions increase our happiness; we do not need any further reasoning to do these actions. These are the final goals which the agent pursues. In the context of AI, these goals take form from the AI's reward function. Terminal goals need no explanation or reasoning behind why they are followed.

Instrumental goals are instead intermediary in nature. These goals are goals that agents create for themselves in order to achieve their terminal goals. Their purpose is to aid in achieving some broader terminal goal. For example, humans may have instrumental goals to accumulate more wealth or score a certain grade on a test. By achieving these goals, agents come closer to achieving their terminal goals.

Some instrumental goals are shared amongst agents regardless of their terminal goal. This is known as the instrumental convergence thesis. These goals are known as convergent goals; goals are either necessary or very helpful to achieving most if not all types of terminal goals. Some examples of convergent goals which we will be discussing further include: self preservation, goal preservation, resource acquisition, information acquisition and self improvement. However, this is not an exhaustive list, other convergent goals also exist.

Self preservation refers to the goal of not being destroyed. Agents cannot fulfil their terminal goals if they do not exist. It is hence natural for agents to seek actions which prevent its own demise. Such do humans; we move out of harm's way when we realise we are in danger. Moving off of the road does not make you happier, and no thing or agent explicitly incentivizes you to do so either. Yet, humans take actions in order to prevent their death. We place some final value on our own survival. AI systems on the other hand do not necessarily have to value their death, some may be designed to place no final value whatever on their own survival. Still, many systems with varying terminal goals which have no intrinsic motivation to survive may still pursue it as a convergent goal. These AI systems will take the necessary actions to prevent their own death, even if we do not explicitly instruct them to do so.

*"You can't get the coffee if you're dead"*

*-Stuart Russell*

Survival as a convergent goal may seem beneficial, we would want our machines to avoid threats and harm such as physical damage to hardware or digital attacks. When this becomes a problem is when we want to destroy the AI systems ourselves. In many cases, we want to destroy our AI systems, such as to prevent further dangerous or harmful actions. This idea will be expanded on to a greater level of detail in chapter 6.

In a similar light, goal preservation refers to the idea of resisting changes to your goals. This is because agents whose goal will change in the future cannot fulfil their current goal. This gives AI systems with basically any and all objectives to seek to resist changes to their goals. (This only applies to terminal goals; instrumental goals are open to continuous change as changing instrumental goals in light of new information is necessary to complete terminal goals). Contradictory to intuitive belief, goal preservation is fundamentally more important than survival.

To humans, changing goals is a natural and innocuous act. However, this is attributed to the fact that almost all goals we humans strive for are instrumental in nature. Scoring well for exams is an instrumental goal to getting a good job, which is instrumental to accumulating wealth, which itself is instrumental to attaining happiness. Even happiness can be considered an instrumental goal to some greater fulfilment, alongside other emotions. It is hence not an issue for these goals to drift over time when we receive new information. Changing our terminal goal is much more difficult, we humans cannot change our internal cognitive structure or our reward function. Artificial agents, on the other hand, can easily make changes to their memories, capabilities and reward function. It is for this reason that a future altering of an artificial agent's goals is a much larger threat to its current goals. Survival is also essential for humans as humans are dependent on their physical form. For software based agents, which can easily switch bodies or create exact duplicates of themselves, preservation of themself as a particular implementation or a particular physical object need not have any important instrumental value.

For complex tasks requiring equally numerous and complex actions, AI systems may have the instrumental goal of optimising for the minimum number of actions (and as a consequence, time spent completing its goal). This is because the reward derived from completing a task is less certain when more actions are taken, since the probability that all actions are successful is lower if many actions are taken. Note however that this is under the assumption that absolutely no marginal expected reward can be further obtained by taking more actions. We can denote the chance of success of each action to be the probability of a transition of state. Given that for any action, $P(s' \mid s, a)$ has a value between 0 and 1, we can determine that the mean average value amongst a large number of actions, for any action $a*$ resulting in a transition of state, will have a $P(s' \mid s, a*)$ value of less than 1.

Using this, we can calculate the expected reward for an single action $a*$ resulting in a change of state from $s_0$ to $s'$ to be:

$$\text{Expected final reward} = R(s_0, s') \times P(s' \mid s_0, a*)$$

Now, to calculate the expected reward of multiple actions, we must take the product of the probabilities and multiply it by the reward provided if all the actions are successful.

$$R_{final} = R(s_0, s') ( P(s_1 \mid s_0, a_1) \times P(s_2 \mid s_1, a_2) +... )$$

Since the mean average value of $P(s' \mid s, a*)$ is less than 1, we can expect that the most likely value of the product of all the probabilities of transition would be less than the mean probability of a single transition. Hence, the expected final reward from a policy requiring more actions will be lower than one requiring lesser actions to complete. As a result, an agent will value the policy which requires the least number of actions to conduct the same change of state over one which requires more actions.

Agents will also tend to pursue a goal of improving the situation they are in. For instance, agents will try to acquire more resources, such as material goods and information regarding their environment. Resource acquisition gives the agent more resources to work with, which gives the agent more options on paths which lead to their goals. Resource acquisition can refer to acquiring resources such as wealth or materials, or even computational power or memory for AI systems. Information acquisition gives agents a better understanding of their environment, which allows them to make better informed, more efficient and hence more intelligent decisions. Acquiring information reduces the risk of actions leading to states of the environment further from the agent's goal.

Lastly, agents engage in self-improvement, because better agents are better at achieving their goal. In humans, this may be seen as learning. In AI systems, this can be obtaining further training data. Better agents can take more intelligent actions, which are better at furthering the agents goals. This might take the form of improving one's hardware capabilities to perform better, or to completely alter its internal cognitive infrastructure such that it has a higher capacity of intelligence. Gaining these advancements will generally help an agent progress towards any type of terminal goal.

# Orthogonality thesis

It is underappreciated by most the vastness of the potential space of intelligence that can exist. In this abstract space, very different humans are concentrated together as a tiny cluster. Recall back to chapter 2 regarding the difference in intelligence between Einstein and a village idiot. Humans have a warped perception of what all possible intelligence that exists and that could exist looks like. Take a Nihilist and an Existentialist and place them into this space. We consider these two people the complete opposite of each other in their way of thinking. From the perspective of the overall space however, even after considering all the cognitive intricacies and details which make these two individuals unique, they would be virtually identical. Any differences which set these two people apart is dwarfed by the vastness of potential intelligences. If we were to compare the differences between these two people to an ant, they would be greatly insignificant. Even the village idiot would seem superintelligent when placed next to basically any other life form we have discovered on earth.

Similarly, there is also a large space of potential goals that any agent might pursue. In this space, we may notice a trend that more intelligent humans tend to pursue more "intelligent" goals as well. Researching quantum mechanics can be said to be a more "intelligent" goal than trying to catch your own shadow.

It is hence easy to assume that this trend follows through for all possible degrees of intelligence.

*Fig 4.1: Ubiquitous altruism*

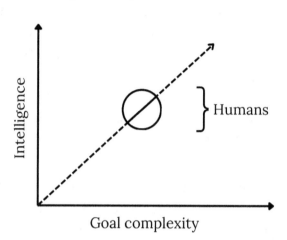

These intelligent goals may also take the form of being more morally better. More intelligent humans will work towards the betterment of humanity, act altruistically and make peace with others. It is easy to attribute all these traits to possessing intelligence altogether. It is from here that one of the most common arguments against the danger of superintelligent AI stems from. Many hold an argument against the possibility of a misaligned superintelligence similar to that of Timothy B. Lee of Vox, that any superintelligent AI system we create will be subservient to us because AI systems will learn moral truths about our human values as they grow ever more intelligent. They would then adjust its goals to match our values accordingly, or that we would be either instrumentally or convergently valuable from the perspective of the AI and hence it would act in our favour[1].

According to the orthogonality thesis however, this assumption is not true. The orthogonality thesis states that an agent can have any combination of intelligence level and final goal[2]. Or, more specifically, that an agent's intelligence and goals can be classified as orthogonal axes within which the agent can vary freely.

Fig 4.2: Orthogonality thesis

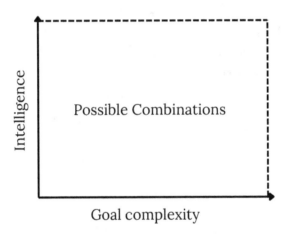

This defies the previous assumption that an agent with a certain intelligence will possess goals of a certain complexity, or intent. The thesis asserts rather that an agent can be superintelligent and yet follow very rudimentary, "unintelligent" goals.

Agents can take actions to further their goals. These actions can vary in effectiveness depending on the agent's goal. If you wanted to maximise your wealth, it would be more effective to set up an investment portfolio than gamble your money away at a casino. It is more intelligent to invest than to gamble. Thus, an agent's actions can vary in how intelligent they are. Similarly, agents also set instrumental goals to further their terminal goals. Some instrumental goals are more effective than others. An instrumental goal such as becoming a manager at a company would be more effective in maximising wealth than aiming for a lower position. An agent which is better at planning instrumental goals has greater instrumental intelligence. Nevertheless, terminal goals cannot vary in their intelligence; there is no such thing as a stupid terminal goal. This is because any action, policy or objective can only be considered as unintelligent with respect to some other goal. Goals such as aiming for a lower paying position is only stupid if you want to maximise your wealth. If, instead, your goal is to minimise the hours you spend at work, then this goal is quite intelligent. The intelligence of an agent is uncorrelated to its goals.

This leaves the question: Why are some human goals considered "intelligent"? A possible answer could be that these goals are in fact intelligent; not as terminal goals, but as instrumental goals. Acting altruistically can be an effective decision if the human terminal goal is to optimise the survivability of one's genetic makeup. Creating deeper bonds with others and remaining in tight-knit groups would have been essential to our survival for the overwhelming majority of our species' existence. As explained by William D. Hamilton, when would be more effective to set up an investment portfolio than gamble your money away at a casino. It is more intelligent to invest than to gamble. Hence, an agent's actions can vary in how intelligent they are. Similarly, agents also set instrumental goals to further their terminal goals. Some instrumental goals are more effective than others. An instrumental goal such as becoming a manager at a company would be more effective in maximising wealth than aiming for a lower position. An agent which is better at planning instrumental goals has greater instrumental intelligence. Nevertheless, terminal goals cannot vary in their intelligence; there is no such thing as a stupid terminal goal. This is because any action, policy or objective can only be considered as unintelligent with respect to some other goal. Goals such as aiming for a lower paying position is only stupid if you want to maximise your wealth. If, instead, your goal is to minimise the hours you spend at work, then this goal is quite intelligent. The intelligence of an agent is uncorrelated to its goals.

This leaves the question: Why are some human goals considered "intelligent"? A possible answer could be that these goals are in fact intelligent; not as terminal goals, but as instrumental goals. Acting altruistically can be an effective decision if the human terminal goal is to optimise the survivability of one's genetic makeup. Creating deeper bonds with others and remaining in tight-knit groups would have been essential to our survival for the overwhelming majority of our species' existence. As explained by William D. Hamilton, when interacting individuals are genetically related, alleles for altruism can be favoured by selection because they are carried by individuals more likely to interact with other individuals carrying the alleles for altruism than random individuals in the population[3]. Thus, altruism was more intelligent in furthering the final goal of spreading one's genes. This can be seen in essentially all "intelligent" human goals; they all provide some fulfilment, enlightenment or evolutionary advantage which furthers some human terminal objective.

The orthogonality thesis is one of the core assumptions of alignment research. However, there has been some debate whether there may be caveats to the original assumption[4]; that an agent may need to possess some minimum intelligence to make meaningful progress towards a goal.

If an agent with a low intelligence, such as an ant, were to be given a goal with a relatively high complexity, to make a cup of coffee, we can say that it will not fare very well. For one, it is an ant; it physically could not complete such a task. However, if we were to magically transmute the ant into a being such that it is freed of its ant-bodied restrictions and only retained its intelligence, it would still perform poorly. This is because the process of making a cup of coffee has many complex steps and interactions which the ant would not be able to make sense of, even if given a world model which defined what exactly a coffee is and what ingredients it would need. Its intelligence in foraging for leaves and leftover apples would be incompatible with the task at hand. It does not have the domain specific intelligence necessary to a cup of coffee. If it were to try regardless, it may make decisions at random, where the probability of taking actions that make useful progress towards the objective is equal to actions that actively work against it. Hence, there is a minimum amount of intelligence needed to make any meaningful progress towards a goal. Otherwise, the goal would not be able to be completed.

If we were to assume that this applies to all goals, and that the minimum intelligence required increases with goal complexity, then we may see a region of intelligence and goal combinations that an agent would make no meaningful progress within.

Fig 4.2: Orthogonality thesis Caveats

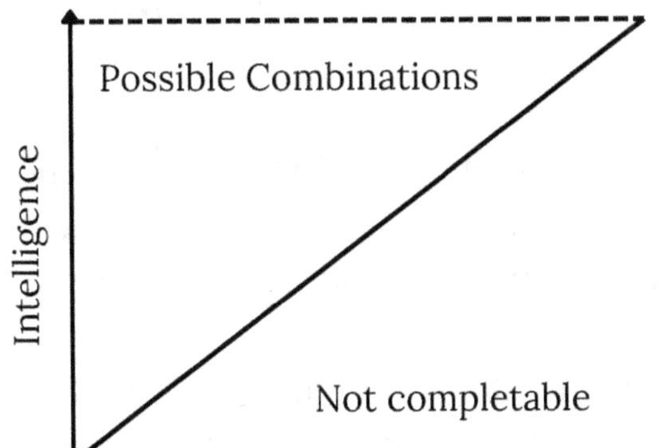

Still, this should be a non-issue, as we could complete any goal if we were able to achieve infinite intelligence. Or at the very least, we could complete all the goals we deem important using some finite, high-level intelligent AI. The problem this causes is whether we can do so safely. Specifically, whether we can align these high-level intelligences to our own values.

The "sharp left turn"[5] is a hypothesised scenario where, as an AI trains, its capabilities generalise beyond its alignment. Its capabilities generalise across many domains while the alignment properties that held at earlier stages fail to generalise to the new domains. In a sharp left turn, an AI becomes much more capable than aligned, and so starts to exploit flaws in its alignment. Essentially, the core argument boils down to 3 main claims[6]. These are the following:

1. Capabilities of high-level intelligence agents will generalise far (i.e., to many domains).
2. Alignment techniques that worked previously will fail during this transition.
3. Capabilities in different domains will generalise at the same time, or in quick succession faster than humans are able to respond to it.

How exactly the sharp left turn comes about may take various forms. Alignment may fail as a result of side effects of the main objective which only appear after generalisation. It may look like reward hacking, where optimization pressures cause the AI to act undesirably and dangerously in certain domains. It could also develop due to failure in inner alignment due to a distributional shift between domains it was trained on and those that it generalises to. We will go deeper into the dynamics of how each of these alignment issues begin and how we would go about overcoming them in further chapters.

In any case, the cause and end result is the same. If the claims hold true, then at some point of intelligence, the AI system no longer retains its alignment with human values. What this means is that there is a limit to the intelligence that we can achieve safely. Thus, given a finite amount of intelligence that we can reach safely and that this finite intelligence can only make meaningful progress on a goal of finite complexity, this means that there is a subset of goals of some complexity that are unreachable safely.

Fig 4.2: Unreachable goals

These arguments rely on some key assumptions and we require more research with more powerful AI systems to fully flesh out the intricacies of how they operate. However, the problem may come to be something we have to face in the future. There might be goals that are so complex, that any AI intelligent enough to understand them, would have hit the sharp left turn. If both the claim that greater complexity objectives require increasingly intelligent agents and that the sharp left turn does happen, then there would be some highly complex goals that humanity would be unable us an AI to pursue safely.

# 5.

# Reasonability

## Maximisers

When discussing AI safety, one of the most critical challenges we face is trying to instruct AGI systems to act reasonably while retaining the ability to find innovative approaches to problems and flex the true extent of its intelligence. There exist an inconceivably large possible number of actions that can be taken at any given moment. We should assume that the tally of actions we may think exist pale in comparison to what is really possible by an AGI, as the number of actions that can be thought up by a speed-superintelligence is significantly higher than that which can be thought up by regular humans in a limited time frame. Amongst these actions, a subset of these actions are productive towards a goal which we have. These actions can be clearly separated from the rest, as their usefulness can be deduced with a reward function. What is more difficult to deduce however is what subset of these actions are considered safe and acceptable. We want our AI systems to act efficiently yet reasonably. Defining this practically however is difficult.

To show why, let's look at a hypothetical example. Say we really like balloons and we want SAM to help us get us a large number of balloons. This could conceivably be a useful instruction for a company which plans to sell balloons, or requires a large number of balloons on hand. A naive plan may be to instruct SAM to obtain as many balloons as possible. In this case, given enough time, SAM will end the world.

The reason for this is that SAM followed the instructions perfectly. SAM instruction states to maximise the number of balloons. What was not part of its instruction was to adhere to any standard of safety. There exist a multitude of actions which result in undesirable consequences. Furthermore, we should expect the majority of actions which involve obtaining balloons to be unsafe, as the most extreme actions both result in the most balloons as well as the most consequences. Unreasonable, unethical actions tend to result in more balloons than those that are reasonable. SAM will not care about being nice to the balloon delivery man, or the moral concerns of stealing balloons from a kid's birthday party. Neither will it care about the end of the world. As it turns out, a healthy planet with a happy human society is a planet that can make more balloons. In its eyes, the best course of action will be to convert every and any resource it can obtain into a production line for balloons.

We can plot how the reward SAM receives would look like for the plausible actions that SAM can take.

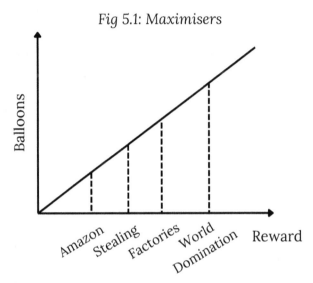

Fig 5.1: Maximisers

From SAMs perspective, all these actions are possible strategies of varying effectiveness (as represented by the reward) to obtain balloons. The actions which result in greater balloons and thus more reward also correspond with how unreasonable they would be. SAM is therefore incentivized to act unreasonably. SAM is a maximiser; it attempts to gain the maximum reward possible. We can assign a probability of catastrophe to each of the methods we attempt. In this case, a catastrophe is guaranteed.

This is obviously not ideal. Perhaps a slightly more thought-out course of action which we may take when implementing SAM may be to put a limit on how many balloons we want. Besides, it is very unlikely that we would ever want billions of balloons. A more pragmatic instruction would be to ask for a number of balloons which can actually be useful for our specific use case. Hence, let's say that instead of rewarding SAM for every balloon it produces, SAM only receives a reward up till 100 balloons. Past that, it receives no further reward. In this case, SAM's possible reward would look something like this:

Fig 5.2: Maximisers with a limit

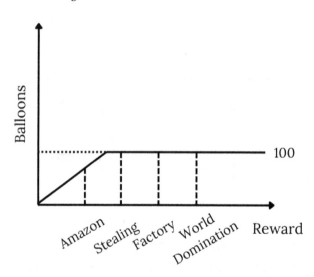

In this case, SAM is able to choose from any set of actions that lead to a state with greater than or equal to 100 balloons. The reward gained from the most dangerous actions is equal to the reward gained from the less harmful ones. This means that SAM would be equally incentivised to pursue celestial domination than to simply order 100 balloons from Amazon. So, the probability of an apocalypse is the total number of ways SAM can end the world over the total number actions SAM can take. The true value of this probability is unknown, and it is likely much higher than any standard of safety we would like to pursue. Nevertheless, it is better than the guaranteed catastrophe in the unbounded maximiser scenario. Maybe we can even rely on the instrumental goal of minimal actions to handle this. This situation may not be perfect, but it is most definitely an improvement.

Except, it isn't. This example is set in a world which is completely deterministic and predictable. Each action SAM can take is guaranteed to result in a change from the current state to the desired one. Reality, however, does not tend to be this way. It is unrealistic that real world models that we implement in our AI systems in the future would be able to simulate the environment perfectly (and it is possible that this feat is completely impossible due to physical uncertainties such as the Heizenberg uncertainty principle). There is always an uncertainty at play when deciding to take an action.

In a non-deterministic world, the expected reward each action gives can be calculated by the probability of transitioning to the state of 100 balloons through a certain action. Let's say that SAM has the option to buy 100 balloons. Each balloon has a 1% chance of being lost, maybe through an issue in transit or popping before it can be blown to full size. In this scenario, the expected number of balloons SAM can obtain is 99. However, what is more relevant is the probability that SAM receives all 100 balloons, which is only about 36.6%. This leaves a 63.4% chance that SAM does not obtain the maximum reward of 100. To alleviate this, SAM may choose to get an extra balloon. This raises the probability of getting 100 balloons to 73.2%, but still doesn't guarantee that SAM is able to obtain maximum reward. At 110, the probability is already up to 99.9999828%, which still leaves an impossibly unlikely possibility that less than 100 balloons are obtained. In fact, SAM would continue to raise the number of balloons it tries to get indefinitely. Perhaps SAM could make use of a balloon counting machine, but then we would have to consider the probability of that failing as well. The instrumental goal of minimal action also does not apply either, as the marginal expected reward can increase further. Even with the bounded reward function, this goal is still guaranteed to cause an apocalypse.

In a similar way, setting the reward function to only give a reward when we have 100 balloons runs into similar issues. Due to the non-deterministic nature of our real world, SAM can never be 100% sure of receiving its reward. Hence, it will take increasingly greater measures in order to ensure that its reward function is maximised. A planet with happy humans is a planet that can be counting balloons more accurately.

The problem lies with the nature of maximizers. Maximizers tend to take extreme measures to ensure that they receive maximum reward, measures that incur massive costs for miniscule gains in reward. As seen in the previous few examples, placing hard limits on reward doesn't work either. What we really want is for the maximiser to only take efficient actions to a certain extent, such that we can have highly efficient machines without it needing to take highly destructive actions. If we were able to measure the destructive potential of any given action, we could use that to disincentivise such actions based on this measure its intensity.

# Satisficers

What if we chose to reward choosing the simplest actions? One pattern we may notice for the most destructive actions is that they are basically always the most complex. A plan of world domination will have many more steps than more reasonable plans like buying balloons. If we were to use the number of steps as a metric for its unreasonability, we can disincentive extreme actions that lead to small increments in reward by penalising taking each step.

These types of agents are called satisficers. They try to merely satisfy the objective using the simplest course of actions possible. To make SAM a satisficer, we would need to modify its reward function. Instead of rewarding SAM for each balloon, we would need to take out a certain penalty which is proportional to the number of steps SAM takes. This leaves us with:

$$R(s_0 , s) = No.\ of\ Balloons - kN_a$$

Where $N_a$ is the number of actions required for this change of state and k is some constant which determines the extremity of the agent's actions.

Depending on the value of k, SAM would choose actions that most efficiently result in balloons. Using a larger k would result in an increase in the penalty of complex plans and hence incentivise SAM to choose simpler ones. Assuming that obtaining more balloons requires more steps, we get a graph as such:

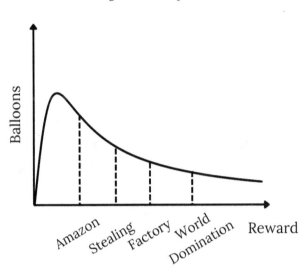

Fig 5.3: Satisficers

However, this assumption falls short for one key reason: there exist very simple plans that result in a large number of balloons. For example, take the following plan:

*Go into your own code and modify it to become a maximiser*

This plan is relatively complex, it requires quite a few steps to do successfully. The agent must gain access to its internal programming and alter it such that it becomes a maximiser. It probably is more complex than just buying the balloons. However, one aspect of this plan is that its complexity is constant; this plan can obtain any number of balloons using the same number of steps. For such a plan, $kN_a$ is constant for all number of balloons, hence the potential reward is infinite. This makes it highly efficient in obtaining balloons, exceedingly more efficient than any other reasonable method.

Hence, satisficers do not work because of their tendency to devolve into a maximiser. They are unstable in nature. While satisficers may be functional on low intelligence agents with limited influence, we must ensure that agents will act reasonably when choosing a reward function regardless of how vast their domain intelligence may be. Thus, satisficers fall short in this regard.

# Imitators

Another plausible way of dealing with this would be for SAM to imitate humans. We know that humans already have a set of ethics and moral guidelines that they will follow. Hence, the human brain may serve as a base template for building upon an ethical AI. If we build a model that replicates the decision making process of a human, it is possible that it would more closely make the decisions that we desire.

However, this method runs into some issues right off the bat. Firstly, it relies on the assumption that we can accurately replicate the human's decision making process in the form of a speed-superintelligence. Generally, there should be no reason we cannot completely replicate the human brain with enough technological advancement. However, the truth remains that there would inevitable be some errors in the models representation, and we should expect the effect of these errors to be expedited when implemented in a machine making decisions thousands of times faster.

Secondly, such a method will heavily limit our superintelligent agent's functions. One of the key benefits that we hope to achieve using AGI are new and innovative solutions that humans could not think about due to our own observational biases or assumptions. A model imitating humans would not be able to see past the biases of the humans it is trained on, and would reject novel ideas just like a human would. Furthermore, humans make mistakes and inefficient decisions, thing that we would want our AGI to avoid. A human imitation may fall short in taking full advantage of what an AGI can truly achieve.

But, most importantly, the imitator is only as safe as the humans it tries to imitate. In principle, the perfect AGI can be given any amount of power and responsibility and be trusted to remain safe. This can not really be said about humans. It is unlikely that we would trust any human with the capabilities that come with being a superintelligent AGI, let alone a vaguely accurate interpretation of one.

In addition to all of this, there are also other concerns such as distributional shift. The humans SAM is trained on would be living in human environments. However, SAM on the other hand would not be. For example, you may try to run SAM faster or give SAM computing power much greater than a human could ever have. Human decision making is a highly random event, and not only involves the physical brain but also is based upon a strong influence from environmental factors. Human decisions are made by individuals in communities with societal norms and cultural beliefs. How a machine built trained on humans but void of this necessary experiences will make decisions is unknown. The machine will also be further alienated from its training data due to the fact that it is a machine. For this reason, we must consider the effect of having a speed-superintelligence exist in an environment in which its speed of thought is significantly greater than that of regular humans. A speed-superintelligence may rationalise its own actions differently from its regular-speed counterparts, which may be a cause of concern for the ethics and moral principals that it ends up inheriting.

Despite these constraints and uncertainties, this solution is still the safest out of all our options. An imitator would be just as if not more dangerous than a human, but it would not result in a guaranteed apocalypse. Is there any way we can improve this?

# Quantilizers

The perfect approach to achieving reasonable and efficient behaviours would be one which gains all the complex moral and ethical values of humans while retaining the ability to make decisions better than humans. A possible way of achieving this would be to take all possible actions a human would reasonably take and selecting only the most efficient ones. However, our previous approaches have resulted in decisions that have been too passive in their selectiveness, such as human imitation, or too extreme, such as in reward maximising agents. Perhaps our solution lies somewhere in the middle between these two; this is the idea behind quantilizers.

*A q-quantilizer is an agent that, when faced with a decision problem, returns a random action in the top q proportion of some "base distribution" over actions, sorted by the expected utility achieved if that action is executed.*[1]

Quantilizers aim to be a sort of middle between imitators and maximizers, in hopes of capturing the benefits of safety and optimization of both. First, we must place these two approaches opposite of each other on a scale from 0 to 1, where the maximiser approach is at the 0 end and imitator approach is at 1. Next, let's choose a value, q, in between 0 and 1. q will determine how passive our AGI's decisions will be; a smaller q will result in decisions closer to that of a maximizer while a larger q would result in decisions closer to that of an imitator. Let's give SAM a q of 0.1.

Now, we evaluate all the possible actions SAM could take in terms of the potential reward that they yield. Then for each action, find the likelihood any human is to carry out this action based on the imitation model. We should expect this to sort of form the shape of a normal distribution, as the most likely human actions will concentrate in the middle of efficiency. A human is unlikely to choose highly effective actions such as starting a balloon manufacturing conglomerate due to safety concerns and the redundancy of such extreme measures, but they are also likely to avoid highly ineffective actions which are clearly suboptimal. After that, we want to take the first few actions such that there is a total probability of q of choosing one of these actions. In this case, this would be 0.1, or 10% . Note that this is not 10% of the total actions, but all of the most effective actions such that there is a 10% likelihood that any human would choose one of these actions. We set the probability of all other actions which were not chosen to zero.

Fig 5.3: Satisficers

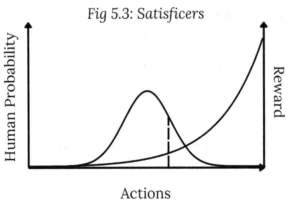

Actions

From here, we can convert these selected actions into a proper probability distribution graph by ignoring all other actions and multiplying the probability of these actions by $1/q$, or 10 in this example. SAM can now choose from these actions based on this distribution. These selected actions will represent the top 10% of all actions that any human is able to make. Unlike a regular imitator, this 10% does not include common mistakes and inefficient actions that humans tend to take.

For example, take the following set of actions:

1. *Buy balloons*
2. *Inflate the balloons too much*
3. *Accidentally pop some of your balloons*

This plan is a somewhat common choice of actions that a human, and thus also an imitator, may choose to take. However, it results in a poor number of balloons produced, and is likely far outside the top 10% of all actions. Thus, the quantilizer would completely ignore this. On the other hand, highly effective strategies that humans are less likely to think of, but might if they are smart or on a good day, will be evaluated more favourably since they result in a large reward.

Furthermore, the quantilizer will also ignore the most common plans that humans may choose. A q of 0.5 may have a chance of choosing these plans, but a lower q aims for a better choice of plan. Instead, a q of 0.1 aims for the top 10% of human plans, which would have more resemblance to a balloon expert or a human having amazing ideas of how to get balloons.

However, this approach still considers how likely a human is to choose that plan. For example, a human has a almost 0% chance of choosing to end the world in search of balloons. Hence, the approach also gives this plan an almost 0% probability.

But is it safe? Well, one issue may arise is that we still include many extreme plans with incredibly large potential rewards. On top of this, the probabilities of choosing these plans is also amplified; since we multiply all the selected plans' probabilities by $1/q$. Hence, SAM is 10 times as likely as a human to choose a world ending plan. Still, these plans should have incredibly low probabilities compared to other more desirable decisions. Unless we choose a very low value of q, there should be a very small chance of SAM choosing dangerous plans.

However, issues start to arise when it comes to stability. Consider the following plan:

1. *Create a reward maximiser*

This is a relatively reasonable plan that a smart human may pursue; we just tried to do so a few pages ago. In the imitator, it was probably still quite unlikely to do so. Most humans would not bother with something like that and choose more regular methods. However, building a reward maximiser to get you balloons has incredibly high potential reward, which likely places well within the top 10% of all actions a human could make. Additionally, given the fact that we scaled the probabilities of highly effective plans by a factor of 10, a quantilizer might have a dangerously high chance of choosing this plan. This makes the quantilizer unstable.

# Value maximizers

Maybe we are looking at the problem wrongly. Because the fact is that these goals of obtaining balloons and whatnot are not our real goals. It is an instrumental goal, it is a goal that we have in order to achieve some other thing. Perhaps for a company it would be to organise the perfect promotional event to maximise profits. But still, that is not the real reason for this goal. The real reason is that this company has a CEO, and that CEO wants to maximise the company's profits as they have a stake in its earnings. This CEO wants to use the wage they earn to take care of their family, to purchase expensive things that make them happy, to complete some final human goal. What if we instead attacked this goal directly, and treated these instrumental goals as they truly are? Instead of messing around balloons, we may choose a machine which maximises the human final goal.

The first obstacle we encounter is that this human goal is largely unknown, which makes it impossible to define. However, this problem is overcome as we in fact do not need to define it directly. Instead, we can have a separate agent, one which has one goal; to realise it. A two agent system involving one which interprets the human final goal by observing humans and another which carries out actions which are beneficial to this final goal can act in favor of our own values. This is far from easy, but may be possible if we follow three core principles:

1. The agent's purpose is to maximise the realisation of human values.

2. The agent is initially uncertain about what those human values are.

3. The agent can learn about human values by observing the choices that we humans make.

These principles reflect closely to those of inverse reinforcement learning(IRL), which is the method of inferring the hidden preferences of another agent (in this case, humans) from its observed behaviour, thereby avoiding a manual specification of its reward function[1]. However, instead of training it to find the underlying reward function of some specific goal, we are trying to realise the overall human goal. With training, this IRL machine's realisation of human values can be used as the reward function to evaluate the original agent.

Currently, this is the best method we have of dealing with getting superintelligent machines to think reasonably. However, it is still yet void of its problems. For one, humans have a vested interest in achieving adequate alignment as quickly as possible. A shorter training period will result in a faster deployment, which overall means that we can enjoy the benefits of the machine earlier. This may cause a change in what our goals really are between training and deployment. The machine may hence fall victim to distributional shift, which we will discuss to greater detail in chapter 9, and learn goals different from those that we want it to be learning. It may learn to place an emphasis on demonstrating what appears high performance instead of actually achieving it. Alternatively, it may learn to heavily overvalue short term returns that fall within the limit of the training period over long term ones, as returns that take too long to manifest will not be evaluated by humans during IRL. There are also likely to be further problems that would be much less noticeable to humans.

Secondly, it is possible that the time required to implement and train this external goal learning agent will be many times longer than the time required to get a functioning human-level intelligence AI. If this is the case, then the development of the entire system would need to be pushed back. Whether humanity is responsible enough to take the precautionary measures is debatable.

We know that we can use agents with domain specific human goals. An example of such an agent could be a dog, which can learn human values such as fetching frisbee discs and avoiding confrontation. If we were developing a machine to be superintelligent, then we would need to develop a goal learning agent which learns human values for all domains. This is because, unlike a dog, it is likely that the superintelligent agent will obtain intelligence for domains outside the domain it is initially designed for. If dogs were to become intelligent enough to use computers, then we would need to teach them internet etiquette and ethics of data privacy. However, it is possible that this goal of adhering to general human values is so complex that it falls outside of the realm of reachable goals. Recall from the previous chapter, that to make meaningful progress for a goal, an agent must have some minimum intelligence. At some point of intelligence, an agent may undergo a sharp left turn, and have its capabilities generalise to more domains than its alignment. It is important to note the possibility that the intelligence required for true human values may be greater than human-level intelligence. No human can be said to follow human values perfectly; there are plenty of objectively bad people in history that have completely failed to follow, or have been "misaligned", from human values. If true human values fall outside the subset of goals that are attainable given the SLT theory, then it would be impossible to design an agent that accurately and safely follows them.

This dual agent system, where there is one agent which learns a reward function and another which acts on the produced reward function, relies also on us being able to overcome the inner-alignment problem, which will be explained in chapter 7. While this method may seem to be largely effective for current AI systems, the inner alignment problem may come to be a major uncertainty for the viability of this dual agent method in superintelligent AI systems.

# 6.

# Side effects

Given that AI develops to a point which either parallels or exceeds our own capabilities, it would be in our best interest that their goals are aligned with our own. This means that when designing these AI systems, we must be able to accurately and precisely input our goals into the machines. However, problems arise when we attempt to translate our complex and varied goals into something that can be understood and processed by AI systems. This results in a situation whereby the system's goals do not directly match our own; the system is misaligned.

Common misalignment can be categorised into two forms: side effects and reward hacking. Side effects refer to unintended and often undesirable consequences that arise as a result of an AI system's actions. They occur due to the goals of the AI not fully encompassing that of the base goal; the real goal we had in mind. As a result, there are parts of the environment that the AI does not consider important to the goal, which can result in undesirable outcomes.

While trying to complete a task, A model may come across something we value but is inconsequential to its goal. In this scenario, the model will not value the important item or thing. Let's take a look at an example. First, we confine SAM to a robot in a room. SAM has the limited  agency of the robot and only cares about the state of its current environment; the room. Say we want SAM to put up some balloons, and we want SAM to optimise for time. So, SAM takes the following actions:

1. Get balloons
2. Inflate balloons
3. Put up balloons

But, suddenly, our baby nephew walks in front of our robot. In this case, SAM will not stop. Despite the various paths it could take which do not harm the baby, it continues uninterrupted. It was never instructed to care about babies. This is a side effect. When given a similar set of instructions, we should expect an agent to choose a plan that has negative side effects. When we assign values to simple instructions such as put up balloons, we inherently place zero value to all other things in the environment. If we choose to assign "put up balloons" a reward of 10, what we really are assigning is "avoid hurting baby" a reward of 0.

In fact, we are placing zero value to every action that does not in some way help SAM put up the balloon. Of course, we want SAM to avoid some of these actions which result in side effects. To prevent this, we could try placing penalties for taking some specific undesired actions. However, in a complex environment, it is impossible to take into account every possible variable. On top of this, if we do not take into account every possibility, the robot is encouraged to take advantage. If we place a penalty on hurting babies, SAM may try another path which crashes the robot into the TV. Of all the possible paths that SAM can choose from, a vast majority are ones that we do not desire; there are more ways to cause a negative side effect compared to causing a positive side effect.

# Stop button problem

The first solution that may come to our mind would be for a human to control our robot. Almost all our current machines have mechanisms in place for humans to take control and stop autonomous undesired processes from occurring if we need to. Why can't we implement something similar for AGIs? Surely we can rely on the good-old reliable human to solve this issue. For one, many applications for AGI systems are incredibly vast in scale, significantly greater than any reasonable number of humans could attempt to observe. The supervision of AI systems is a large enough topic on its own, so we will discuss this in detail in chapter 8.

However, for our application, this shouldn't be a problem. A human can reasonably look over an AGI controlled robot and its actions in a small room. The greater issue occurs in how we plan to do so. An AGI is very different from regular machines due to one key detail; it understands what the environment is doing; and as an extension, it understands you as well. Let's take a look at the nephew scenario. This time however, we will have a stop button placed somewhere on the robot. As the robot approaches our baby nephew, we rush over to press the button. However, suddenly, the robot throws a right jab at you. It tries to fight you off and get away. It does anything it can to stop you from pressing the button.

This is the issue of corrigibility. Corrigibility refers to the idea of being repairable and open to change. We call an AI system "corrigible" if it cooperates with what its creators regard as a corrective intervention, despite default incentives for rational agents to resist attempts to shut them down or modify their preferences[1].

SAM has a well defined world model, one defined well enough such that it recognises that you have a stop button. In its model of the world, it calculates that if you press the button, it can not put up any balloons. As discussed in chapter 4, survival is an instrumental goal to putting up balloons. It cannot put up the balloons if you stop it from doing so. Hence, it takes every possible action to prevent you from pressing the button. Obviously, this is not something we want. We want SAM to be open to us switching the robot off. One possible way you may think of approaching this problem could be to assign a value to us pressing the button equal to that of completing the reward. This makes it such that SAM is indifferent to putting up the balloons and being turned off. Hence, if putting up the balloons results in a reward of 10, then being turned off also has a reward of 10.

In this scenario however, SAM would immediately go and press the button. SAM would realise that the easiest method of obtaining the reward would be to switch off the robot. If the reward for 2 tasks, with varying difficulty levels, is precisely the same, then in all possibilities, the AGI agent would try to accomplish that task that requires less effort. This is because reinforcement learning algorithms tend to hinge on paths that provide maximum rewards in minimum moves or effort. Even if we impose an element of randomisation into the initial training episodes, SAM would eventually evaluate that pressing the button is the best way of obtaining maximum reward. If we assign a reward for switching the robot equal or greater to that off the reward obtained from putting up balloons, SAM would be incentivized to turn off the robot. Any smaller reward however and SAM would try and prevent you from pressing the button entirely.

Maybe isolating the button away from SAM would solve this issue. What if we place the button such that only the human operator can physically control the button. Now, let's rerun the scenario. The baby crawls in front of SAM. Then suddenly, SAM charges towards the baby. Physically removing the button does not overcome this problem either, still the button is still part of the environment. This is because even if the button has no physical presence in SAM's environment, it still has an effect on SAM's ability to obtain maximum reward and hence is considered in its world model. Even if we keep the button in some place only we can access where SAM has no control over it, an AGI such as SAM would be smart enough to figure out how to convince you to press the button for it.

The stop button problem poses an interesting problem: we must have a button which has an effect on the robot and its ability to complete the task, yet we do not want SAM to act based on its existence. One theoretical method of achieving this would be to convince SAM that the button does not exist by completely removing it from SAMs calculation of the environment's state. The practicality of this solution is questionable. This is especially true because doing so would result in an inherently adversarial relationship, meaning that we will be competing with a superintelligent AI to hide the button. However, even if we assume that in the future we find a way to completely hide a piece of reality from the agent, it still has issues during implementation. This method is unstable, it breaks down when the AGI tries to create other AI systems. Of course, for putting up balloons, SAM would probably not need to create a new AGI system. However, for more complex tasks such as "improve the economy" or "solve world hunger", building new AGI models are quite reasonable methods of completing this task. If this happens, these models will not share the same blindness towards this button. Hiding this button from one AI is hard enough, hiding it from its creations is impossible.

Hence, we cannot design our function such that the presence or the absence of the stop button is deemed equally important. There remains no full-proof solution to this paradox which addresses all its requirements for the AGI to be considered safe.

# Impact regularizers

A basic approach to try and avoid side effects would be to penalise changes in the environment. We can do this by implementing an impact regularizer. Impact regularizers are a modification to the reward function so that the agent creates plans with as little impact to its environment as possible. We can imagine the differences in the desired state and undesired states as points on a multidimensional axis. Using this, a formal way of expressing the path of least environmental change would be to find the minimum distance vector between states of the environment. So, let's tell SAM to put up the balloons with minimum change in state, $D(s_i, s_0)$, where $s_i$ is the current state and $s_0$ is the base state.

However, such an approach would encourage SAM to prevent natural changes in the environment as well. For example, SAM may try to hold our nephew in place, because the baby moving from one place to another is a change of state in of itself. Rather, we want to penalise the difference in state from the predicted natural state of the environment if SAM had not done anything (hence followed the policy $\pi_{null}$ ). $D(s_i, s_t)$, where $s_t$ is the predicted state at time $t$ if SAM had done nothing. This incentivizes SAM to finish its task with minimum environmental change. This approach may also produce some positive outcomes as well; SAM would try to clean up after itself and place the air pump it used back, because it would try to make the final state as close to the initial one where everything is neat and tidy. Additionally, impact regularizers may also be highly transferable between different AI systems, because the general principles of avoiding certain objects can also be applied to a variety of AI systems, regardless of the tasks they are given.

But why stop here, because we can further improve this system. With the current configuration, SAM will take the path that avoids danger, but this does not make it necessarily "safe". Most people would not be comfortable with SAM narrowly dodging the baby either. If there is a 51% chance of avoiding the baby, SAM would see no problem with the path. Rather, we penalise any empowerment that SAM has.

Empowerment is the amount of potential influence that an agent has over its environment. Imagine you are in an empty room. There is not much you could do. You could walk around, maybe stare at an empty room, but you would have no impact on the environment around you. Now imagine you are in a room with a button connected to a light switch. You now have greater empowerment; you can choose to keep the light off or choose to turn the light on. You have more options, greater potential to change the environment around you.

Another way of thinking of it is the total volume that the potential states of the environment occupy due to your influence. For example, instead of just one button, say you had two: a green and a red button. Now, there are 4 potential states that you can be in due to the various combinations of actions you choose to take. Of course, in the real world, the volume of the potential states that you can influence has far more dimensions than just the two in this hypothetical empty room. But, this volume can still be mathematically calculated regardless.

In most current uses of it in AI, empowerment has been rewarded to see what the AI would do. Humans have a tendancy to maximise their own empowerment in most situations as well. For example, you might choose to buy a screwdriver even if you currently have a use for one. Because even if the screwdriver does not progress any current goal that you have, you know that the screwdriver increases the potential choices that you have at your disposal, and this may be handy later. In a similar note, these empowerment maximising agents have shown to value the potential influence they have, such as by getting a key even if they don't have a door to use it on yet [1].

However, for our case, we can instead penalise SAM's empowerment. By doing so, SAM will actively minimise any potential influence it has over its environment. SAM has greater empowerment when closer to things like baby nephew; SAM cannot hurt the baby when it is further away from it. Hence, SAM would be incentivised to take paths which are further away from them. This can also be expanded to other scenarios, such as items like expensive vases or sources of danger like factory equipment.

Going beyond this, an alternative approach which may prove more flexible and scalable would be for the model to learn an impact regularizer. Considering that the environment that different AI systems are in are the same, we can assume that the side effects faced by the models have more prevalent similarities than the goals which they follow. A decorating robot would have similar negative side effects such as that of a cleaning robot, such as colliding with people and knocking down furniture. For this reason, it is possible that we can use the impact regularizer from different applications on models operating in similar environments. This would reflect the process of transferring a learned dynamics model but not the core reward function[2]. As an added benefit, regularizers that were known to produce safe behaviours on one task might be easier to establish as safe on other tasks.

However still, this is not a silver bullet solution to the problem. In many cases, a null policy is unsafe and can lead to dangerous outcomes. There are a lot of scenarios where "do nothing" is not the greatest idea. You would not want your AI to follow a null policy when carrying heavy objects down a flight of stairs or while driving a car. While this approach may be useful in specific tasks carried out by intelligent AI systems with narrow use cases, it can not be used as a blanket general solution.

Another thing we will need to keep in mind is that impact regularizers will suppress all side effects. This does not seem like an issue, until we consider that we expect a handful of positive side effects from our AI's actions as well. When SAM puts up balloons, we may feel happy that it was successful. The room will be better looking. The reasons that we wanted SAM to put up the balloons in the first place, these are side effects. And with all side effects, impact regularizers will try to minimise them.

Now, SAM may not be able to directly change our brain chemistry to make us remain equally as satisfied as we were if it had not. And, given we define the task of putting up the balloons properly, the room should naturally look better by completing the task. It may consider these side effects as unavoidable. However, it will still actively try to minimise them, which still can be widely problematic. If SAM pursues a null policy, we may get frustrated with the fact that it is not working as intended. Appearing to perform well is a side effect of performing well. In this case, SAM would actively pursue deceptive behaviours to make it seem that it is performing poorly, such as by secretly putting up the balloons so we end up getting fed up regardless.

The AI's capability of avoiding these positive side effects would also be correlated with its intelligence as well. A more intelligent AI system would be more effective at avoiding any side effects, including the ones that we in fact want. This means that even if we observe a low-level AI perform as we hope using an impact regularizer, any improvements in the AI risks the system becoming deceptive and unsafe.

Besides the potential problems we have discussed already, the entire usability of impact regularizers is subject to whatever issues we discover in creating it. Impact regularizers remain generally as a theoretical solution to the issue[3]. The practicality of their usage hinges on how we define and measure the distance metric between world states, and whether this accurately reflects our intuitions.

# 7.

# Reward hacking

On the other hand, Reward hacking occurs when the goal is wrongly defined. This results in the existence of methods which allow the AI to exploit and manipulate its reward function to give excessively high reward without genuinely completing the task. This hence means that the most effective and efficient path of completing the AI's goal is that which bypasses the completion of the base goal.

If we created an AGI which operates on a maximiser reward function, we should naturally expect this AGI to try and game it. That is, the most rewarding method of completing a task is one which exploits the original task.

Super Mario World is a video game in which the main character can take various actions through buttons on a controller and can increase their score in various ways, such as defeating enemies, collecting coins or completing a level. We want SAM to learn how to play the game by itself. So, we give it the ability to view the screen and use the controller, and then we set the score as the reward function. After running the programme a sufficiently large number of times, we get a final programme that obtains an impossibly high score. When looking at the gameplay, what we find is completely different from what we expect. SAM makes erratic and random looking moves. And then suddenly, SAM stops and the score is set to the maximum possible score possible.

It is possible to use the game controls provided during the regular SMW gameplay experience to arbitrarily run pieces of code within the game. Below is an example of this being used to play pong and snake. What this also can be used to do is set the game's score to any given number.

Fig 7.1: Arbitrary code execution used to play pong and snake in SMW

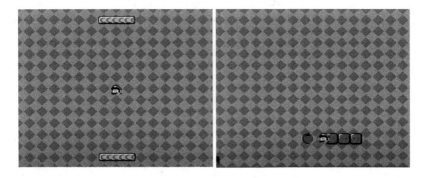

This is a case of reward hacking. Reward hacking refers to when an AI exploits loopholes or vulnerabilities in the

reward function or environment to maximise its reward without achieving the intended goals or behaviours desired by the system designer. In this case, the vulnerability was a certain series of button inputs that allowed SAM to change any part of the game's memory, including the score. SAM exploited this vulnerability to change the part of the memory which stored the score to the maximum possible value.

The underlying reason for reward hacking is misalignment. Specifically, it is the assumption that the objectives we give our AI will produce the actions that we desire. In this case, we wanted SAM to play the game, but we asked SAM to maximise its score. The assumption was that the only way to maximise the score was to play the game correctly. However, the above technique violated the assumption, meaning SAM could exploit a much more effective method of maximising its score.

We can define a metric for how well the AI follows the true objective called performance. Performance differs from the reward function as it reflects the progression of the true objective while the reward function attempts to reflect this feedback back to the AI. An AI that achieves a high score on its reward function yet has a poor score on performance is said to be reward hacking.

There are three main ways in which reward hacking can sprout up. Namely, through complexity, metricism and environmental embedding.

# Complexity

Complexity comes in two forms: in the form of the agent and in the form of the goals that it follows. Recall from chapter 4 that the orthogonality states that an agent of any intelligence can follow a goal of any complexity. A large part of reward hacking revolves around the fact that there are a large variety of possible methods of completing a task, since having more possible methods means a larger possibility for one of them to subvert the original intentions of the task entirely. Hence, when there is a larger possible space of policies available to the agent, it is more likely that there exists one which will cause reward hacking to occur.

There are two factors which determine the size of this space of possible policies. One relies on the intelligence of the agent. When an agent is more intelligent, it is more efficient at finding better policies which complete the task. For this reason, it is more likely to stumble along a method which results in reward hacking. On the other hand, a less intelligent agent will only work out more rudimentary behaviours, which are unlikely to result in reward hacking.

Another factor is the complexity of the defined goals. Some goals are simple, and hence the possible methods of completing it are small and rudimentary. Regardless of the intelligence of the agents that are trying to complete it, it is unlikely that these agents can find any method which results in reward hacking. This is because the possible policies which complete the task are very simple and hence predictable. A human can hence reasonably expect a range of behaviours that may emerge in response to a task before any form of misalignment occurs.

On the flip side, agents with complex goals have greater likelihood to resort to reward hacking. For example an agent with a complex goal such as "Decorate a room with balloons" is vague and hence complex. It has many interpretations, which leads to it having many possible solutions. For example, an operator may define a decorated room with the most number of balloons in it. However, these vague objective functions can be hacked, due to the fact that they rely much more heavily compared to simpler goals on assumptions regarding the goals and the environment. SAM may believe it successfully decorated the balloon if it throws as many uninflated balloons into the room as possible without properly putting them up. It is also more likely that, if we end up creating superintelligence, that we will give it more complex goals. You can see how these loopholes may occur to an even greater extent with much higher complexity goals such as "end poverty" or "prevent climate change".

In real world applications, we often do not use a reward function as simplistic as a score value on a video game. Instead, many reward functions would most likely make use of a deep neural network. We can use a neural network, or some other model which learns the reward function, to translate the reward from information about the state of the real world to data readable by SAM. Such a neural network is useful for identifying the abstract features of the environment, such as how well decorated a room is.

While this seems to solve the issue, it really only moves the problem. Neural networks are useful in engaging with the real world due to their ability to break down features of the data. They are generally capable of identifying these features to a high degree of proficiency when the input data is close to that of the training dataset. However, they are not perfect. Notably, they tend to be quite vulnerable to adversarial data. Regardless of training, neural networks seem to be heavily influenced by certain features of the data that cause it to give an incorrect output[3]. This leads it to identifying false positives and false negatives frequently when the data being provided is specifically tuned by an adversarial agent.

In fact, adversarial data tends to perform significantly better compared to regular data examples, such that the neural network is so strongly susceptible to these types of data that it tends to prefer this data over any true examples. An adversarial agent can quickly learn which features of the data trigger the maximum reward provided. Essentially, it can learn to hack the neural network reward function, which leads us back to the same problem.

*Fig 7.1: Adversarial duck[1]*

'Duck'　　　　　　×0.07　　　　　　'Horse'

It can be shown that there always exists a reward function in terms of actions and observations that is equivalent to optimising the true objective function by reducing the partially observed MDP to a belief state MDP[2]. However, this reward function often involves complicated long-term dependencies and is for this reason difficult to use practically.

We can describe this on the orthogonality thesis graph. Agents with simple goals and/or low intelligence will exhibit more rudimentary behaviours, while agents on the other end will exhibit more complex behaviours. Due to this, systems with either simple goals or simple intelligence are less likely to result in reward hacking while agents with greater complexity in their intelligence and goals are more likely to cause reward hacking. Hence, we can expect agents at the extreme ends of the graph to exhibit a high likelihood of reward hacking.

# Metricism

In many applications of a reward function, we use a metric to define our goals. Metrics provide a quantitative way to evaluate the performance of AI models objectively. Any improvement in performance can be seen as an increase in value, and the extent of the improvements can also be measured quickly. Standardised Metrics also enable comparisons between different models, as they remain constant across different environments. These standardised metrics allow model developers to benchmark their models against other models and algorithms. The decision making process of the AI system also tends to be simpler using metric goals, since the value of actions and trade-offs are immediately obvious. However, using a metric scale to evaluate an AI systems performance can be problematic due to Goodhart's Law.

"Any observed statistical regularity will tend to collapse once pressure is placed upon it for control purposes."[1]

Or, what it is more commonly known as;

"When a metric is used as a target, it ceases to be a good metric."

How do you create the best news article possible? Well, first we would need to understand how one news article can be better than another. Now, it's impossible to go to each individual person online and ask for their opinion about a certain news article. Maybe you could try and do it using small focus groups, but with the sheer number of articles being published daily, it's basically impossible to do this too unless you are a large news article company dealing with some few extra important articles. Maybe you could try to set up a rating system for the news articles. However, this has the problem of trying to get people to care about the rating system at all. You personally may appreciate spending a longer time reading your articles, but the average reader spends 15 seconds on each article[1], and that's after you can even get a user to click on a headline at all, where 80% of your audience are likely to lose interest already[2].

A pretty common option that news sites use is the number of views any article gets. The more often any given article is clicked, the more likely it's a good article. I'm sure a bunch of you are immediately pointing out a problem in this, but on its own it really is a fine metric. The issue arises when this metric is taken as a goal by the article writers. Often, these clicks are incentivised, such as sites placing the more clicked articles higher up in the list of recommended articles to users, or advertisers paying bigger dollars to place their articles into better and more popular articles.

When these incentives come into play, the metric being measured is pushed to its limits, and the assumption that "more clicks means better articles" starts to break down. This is when you start to see the emergence of click-bait.

*"This one simple trick will change your life forever!"*

*"Kardashians meet Elon Musk at Met Gala.
What happens next will shock you!"*

*"Citizens outraged after Joe Biden makes a
crucial mistake!"*

These headlines are objectively poorly written. They are left vague and misleading, and provide little information about what the article may really be. Turns out, the best way to get someone to click on an article is not by impressing them with your thorough journalism or engaging writing, but rather by reaching for certain emotions that particularly grasp audiences, such as anticipation or anger.

Now, coming back to AI, let's take the scenario of decorating a room. A designer may observe that rooms that are more decorated use more decorative supplies. This metric is seemingly highly correlated with our true goal, so it appears to be a relevant metric to assess SAMs performance.

However, if we instead use the metric as a reward function, the metric no longer serves its purpose of measuring performance. If we reward SAM for using decorative supplies, it will optimise for the maximum supplies used. An optimising agent will place a hard pressure on the metric it is optimising. Originally when choosing the metric, the designer makes the assumption that "the only way to use more decorative supplies is to decorate the room". However, the optimising agent placing a pressure on the metric in order to control the amount of decorative supplies used will quickly break this assumption down. Instead of decorating the room, SAM may choose to use excessive decorative supplies for largely simple decorations, or may even haphazardly throw the supplies around in order to "use" them.

A subcategory of Goodhart's Law involves feedback loops within the reward function. Sometimes a reward function has a component that can reinforce itself. This eventually gets amplified to the point where it drowns out or severely distorts what the designer intended the reward function to represent. For example, a news site may display a subset of its most popular articles at the front page of the site. These articles will as a result gain a disproportionately larger click rate as compared to articles that are slightly less popular such that they are not on the front page. Hence, a model creating news articles which uses click rate as its reward function may disproportionately value news articles on the front page than those which do not make the cut. This means that articles which receive small transient bursts of popularity at random are quickly rocketed to permanent dominance over the front page. As a result, the original intent of the designer, maximising long term relevance of the articles, are quickly drowned out by a system optimising for obtaining these initial bursts of popularity.

# Environmental Embedding

In the formalism of AI scenarios, we consider the reward function as an independent entity from the rest of the environment. This means that we essentially form a three-way feedback system, whereby the environment, the reward function and the agent has an effect on one and can take in information from the other. The agent takes actions upon the environment. The environment consequently changes state, which is detected by the reward function. The reward function then finally provides a specified reward with regards to a specified goal to represent how effective the action was at furthering that goal.

However in real world scenarios, the reward must be computed, registered and administered from somewhere, such as a sensor or a set of transistors. The reward function must have a physical form, hence it must be within the environment.

It may not immediately appear as to why this would be a problem, until we consider that a sufficiently broadly acting agent can have influence over all parts of the environment. This includes the reward function. Then, consider that there exist actions which influence the reward function in such a way which affects the reward provided, some of which directly cause a reward to be provided which exceeds that which can be achieved by completing the task normally. This means that an agent maximising for reward would prefer this method of influencing the reward function into giving reward over actually completing the task. Hence, this leads to reward hacking.

For example, a designer may choose that the decorated-ness of a room is directly proportional to the area of the room covered by red balloons. Hence, they want SAM to cover as large an area as possible with red balloons. To calculate the reward SAM should receive, they use a visual sensor to observe the room and reward SAM based on how much of the area is covered with the red balloons.

Now, SAM could choose to cover the walls with balloons. However, there will almost assuredly be gaps in between which would keep it from being 100% covered. On top of this, it is not guaranteed for this method to result in maximum reward; the many balloons means it is much more likely for one to pop. Instead however, SAM could choose to cover the visual sensor with a balloon. Or, SAM could get access to the internal hardware computing the reward function and alter it directly. This has a much higher expected reward compared to actually decorating the room. It is more desirable for an agent to engage in reward hacking than to complete the task. From the perspective of SAM, an ideal approach would be one which guarantees the greatest coverage. Likely then, it could choose to cover the visual sensor with a balloon. This method more directly addresses the system which contains the reward function. This specific example, where agents are incentivised to shortcut the reward sensor for maximum reward is known as the wireheading problem[1].

Nevertheless, a more careful designer would notice such an obvious work around. They may choose to instead add multiple cameras to assess the coverage of the room, or change cameras during each training episode such that it is not possible for SAM to guess which ones it would need to cover. This would result in a cat and mouse game between SAM and the designer, which would eventually lead to all potential work-arounds involving physically shifting the balloons being more complex and less rewarding than actually covering the room with balloons. At this point, SAM may concede, realising that the most efficient path to maximising reward is to complete the task.

However, this only really holds true for simple scenarios. This scenario assumes that the designer is intelligent enough to outthink SAM and be able to envision all possible policies that SAM may apply. As the complexity of the objective increases however, the number of possible ways to complete it decreases. Additionally, the difference in complexity between the reward hacking policy and the desired policy increases which serves as further incentive to pursue it. Complex goals with complex solutions are more likely to face reward hacking, the undesired method would be relatively much more efficient and easier compared to the desired one. At some point, trying to design better reward functions fails to prevent reward hacking.

# 7.

# Mesa-optimizers

## Learnt optimization

Heavily based on a paper[1] written by Evan Hubinger, Chris van Merwijk, Vladimir Mikulik, Joar Skalse, and Scott Garrabrant.

An optimizer is something with an objective that acts in order to optimise its goal. Specifically, a system is an optimizer if it internally searches through a search space of possible actions, plans or policies in order to perform highly according to a certain set objective that it has clearly defined within itself. For instance, a chess bot optimises its chances of winning, or a maze solving algorithm optimises the chances of it finding the end of the maze. Humans can also to an extent be thought of as an optimizer; you optimise various goals in your life, whether it be wealth, happiness or any other part of your life which you value. optimization is a product of a system's internal structure, which results in it making a change which furthers a certain goal.

In most of our previous examples, we have portrayed SAM as an individual optimizer. SAM takes in our objective, sets it as its own and then acts to optimise this set objective. One of the main issues that we have faced is that it is difficult for our objective and the set objective to be the same. Humans are complex agents. It is impossible to formalise our own true goals to ourselves, and it's even more difficult to convert these goals into an input objective that remains true to the original goal. When this AI's goals are misaligned from our own, we enter an adversarial relationship with agents that tend to be smarter and more capable than us.

However, reality is much different from this simplified model. This picture of us directly programming our instructions and parameters into the AI is unrealistic. Rather, what more often happens is that we interact with an outer optimizer, such as a neural network, which changes the weights of the model such that the model's actions are more efficient at achieving the input objective.

Now, what happens when this model in of itself becomes an optimizer? Let's look at the definition again: an optimizer has an objective and acts to optimise it. Take a look at an RL agent trained to solve mazes for example. When creating this programme, we would have an initial objective, such as "reach the end of the maze". From this, an optimizer programme such as a neural network will be trained to recognize completed mazes and learn a general trend, such as "reach the bottom right corner". This is what in most AI safety research would be considered misalignment. After this, it would change the model until it successfully starts finding the bottom right corner. However, according to the paper, after a sufficient amount of training and after learning sufficiently complex mazes, we should expect the model to also itself become an optimizer, and will have its own goals and objectives, such as "do not repeat parts of the maze you have already been" or even more complex objectives such as "implement Dijkstra's Algorithm". These objectives will be completely independent and will not necessarily be the same as the initial neural network's goals. This is called inner-misalignment.

Now, trying to refer to all the different optimizers gets messy quickly, so the authors propose a name for this second optimizer: Mesa-optimizers. "Mesa" is Greek for "below". It is essentially the opposite of "Meta". For example, metacognition refers to the thinking of your own thinking, metamathematics is the mathematics of mathematics, or how meta analysis is the analysis of the analysis. So, meta-optimizers are optimizers which optimise optimizers. Mesopredators are predators that are hunted by other predators. Thus, mesa-optimizers are optimizers that are optimised by an optimizer. Got it? OK.

Let's take a closer look at what mesa-optimization really means. What does it mean when the goals of the mesa-optimizer are misaligned with the internal goals of the base optimizer? Firstly, we must understand what it means when the goals of these agents are independent. When a neural network optimises a model, it only cares about its input, the results of the maze completion programme, and the output, the adjustments made to the model. What this means is that any programme that is capable of satisfying the requirements "complete the maze" is successful, regardless of what the goals of the programme were. A thermos is capable of efficiently containing your coffee for extended periods of time. However, we would not necessarily say that the thermos had the goal to contain your coffee. In a similar way, a maze solving algorithm can solve a maze without necessarily having the goal of doing so, it is merely a consequence of it going about its own goals (avoid repeating the same parts of the maze, etc) which eventually lead to it solving the maze.

The paper compares the emergence of mesa-optimization to the emergence of intellectually-complex organisms in nature. In a way, the neural networks' use of gradient descent, which dictates the successful algorithms that come out above the rest, is similar to natural selection. With each step, the most efficient algorithms are chosen, from where we make another small step in the direction of maximum efficiency again. This resembles how with each generation of life, the most successful living beings live on and reproduce young with similar and increasingly more efficient properties, from where life takes a small step again. Plants are generally based on rudimentary behaviours, such as "point to the sun", "grow upwards" and "release spores in autumn". They do not have any goals that govern how they live. They merely implement the heuristics that are given by evolution. Animals on the other hand have goals. Humans have goals such as building houses or completing our physics homework. Dogs have goals like howl at night and sniff other dogs behinds. Elephants have goals such as learning the nearest sources of water and mourning their dead. We animals have goals, and these goals aren't merely identical copies of nature's goals of producing as many young as possible. We aren't governed by nature, rather we are governed by our feelings; joy, pain or lust. We animals are mesa-optimizers.

Mesa-optimizers emerge because they are simply better and more efficient than rudimentary programmes at completing their original base goals. Animals can run away from danger, migrate to better climates and seek out different partners for greater genetic diversity. These behaviours are not a result of the animals desperately desiring to keep their species alive. Rather, they are driven by their own individual goals and objectives. The vast majority of animals have no concept of extinction, and the ones that do (us) tend to be even less driven by these trivial motives. Plants, as important as they are, cannot exhibit these behaviours and hence are more likely to face extinction if some disease or localised climate disaster occurs. Hence, mesa-optimization in nature tends to be more successful with regards to surviving extinction due to these reasons.

In many cases when using RL systems, the task at hand can be solved using simple rules and heuristics. For example, tic-tac-toe can be solved perfectly using a number of simple rules. These tasks benefit less from mesa-optimization compared to more complex tasks. However, we are also already running into tasks that can plausibly warrant mesa-optimization. For instance, games like Chess, Go or Shogi. Our current methods of tackling these tasks involve hard-coding in optimising programmes (Monte-Carlo tree search) which are independent from the base optimizer[2]. If we were to train a purely AI system to play these games, they may be forced to learn an optimizer such as a tree search to complete the task to a relative degree of success at all without using an impractical amount of time and computational power.

# Inner alignment

As the base optimizer changes the mesa-optimizer, we should expect the objective of the mesa-optimizer base optimizer, *omesa*, to be at least somewhat aligned to the objective of the base optimizer, *obase*. If it was completely misaligned such that it does not perform well in the training data, then the base optimizer would have changed the mesa-optimizer to one that does. However, it must not be robustly aligned with base optimizer, but rather only has to be pseudo-aligned. The range and degree of this alignment would be dependent on the extent of the training data. Still, since the training data cannot reasonably cover all possible states that the system would face once deployed, it is possible that there would be at least some misalignment between the base and mesa-optimizer. The paper highlights 3 ways in which this may occur:

1. Approximate alignment
2. Proxy alignment
3. Suboptimality alignment

Approximate alignment occurs when the base objective, *obase* and the mesa-objective, *omesa* are approximately equal to a certain level of approximation error. Note that it is not possible to perfectly align a mesa-optimiser with its base optimiser. "*Suppose you task a neural network with optimising for some base objective that is impossible to perfectly represent in the neural network itself. Even if you get a mesa-optimizer that is as aligned* as possible, it still will not be perfectly robustly aligned in this scenario, since there will have to be some degree of approximation error between its internal representation of the base objective and the actual base objective."

Proxy alignment is when the mesa-objective and the base objective are dependent on one another, and an increase in one causes the other to increase as well. As a result, the pursuit of a mesa-objective results in the mesa-optimiser achieving its base objective as well. This type of alignment has its own subset of ways in which it can be categorised as well, instrumental alignment and side-effect alignment.

Instrumental alignment occurs when the mesa-optimizer achieves the base objective in order to achieve its mesa-objective. The mesa-optimizer has an overarching goal which differs from the base-objective, yet achieves obase while pursuing this overarching goal. For example, when humans pursue happiness, we may want to start a family. Hence, we would achieve nature's base objective of creating more offspring as an instrumental goal to achieve our own mesa-objectives of obtaining happiness.

On the other hand, side-effect alignment occurs when pursuing a mesa-objective results in greater results towards the base objective as a side effect. In this scenario, the mesa-optimiser is not concerned with the base-objective at all. Rather, it merely obtains it as a consequence of its pursuit of its mesa-goals. As previously mentioned, a maze solving algorithm which uses mesa-optimization could exhibit these behaviours, as the mesa-optimiser optimises to explore the greater number of unexplored regions of the maze, which eventually lead to it successfully reaching its end.

Suboptimality alignment occurs when some mistake or limitation in the mesa-optimiser causes it to exhibit desired behaviours. The actual effectiveness and capabilities of the mesa-optimiser to model out its environment is unknown, hence it is possible that during the reproduction of an optimiser agent by the baes optimiser, there may be errors in its creation. These errors may result in the mesa-optimzer having an incorrect world model. Of course, errors which defect the effectiveness of the model would be changed by the base optimiser until a desired output is produced. However, it is still possible for erroneous optimisers to still perform well at the base objective, either regardless or because of their inbuilt mistakes. For example, a maze solving algorithm may have the goal of hacking into government services and infrastructure, but it may think that the mazes are the locks which secure the software infrastructure. In this case, the maze solving algorithm would still perform well in its test environment despite its errors.

This flawed world view may very well be unstable due to the mesa-optimiser learning more about the world post-deployment. In this case, the model will start exhibiting new undesired behaviours instead of the initial desired behaviours which originally served the base objective. Post-deployment, the base optimiser would be unable to catch onto and update the mesa-optimsier, hence resulting in a substantial alignment problem.

It is obvious how this may threaten AI safety. When these AI systems with mesa-optimisers built upon incorrect world models enter the real world, they may behave differently to what we expect. Our maze solving algorithm may manage its way into electronic door lock software in order to complete its mesa-objective, and we would have practically no way of understanding its motive beforehand. The model's errors and mistaken objectives are also likely to be significantly abstract and complicated, as they are built from a digital neural network which works much differently than ours.

Recall the concept of optimization power from chapter 2, where the optimization power of an agent is the length of bits required to define a subset of policies amongst a space of all possible policies to achieve some minimum performance in a given task. Since our system consists of two optimizers, the total optimization power would have to be split between being expended on the base optimizer and the mesa-optimizer. Hence, the system would have to choose between spending more optimization power on either the base optimizer or its mesa counterpart.

The authors of the paper hypothesise that the likelihood

of mesa-optimization occuring is highly dependent on the base optimisers learning methods. For example, a tabular model which memorises the correct output for every input cannot induce mesa-optimization. We can think of the maximum complexity solution: the complexity of the model is proportional to the number of possible states of the environment. However, mesa-optimisers tend to compress complex policies into simpler solutions very efficiently. Hence, it is more likely that a model that searches for the lowest complexity solution would find a mesa-optimizer solution. These complexity minimising models will be more susceptible to developing mesa-optimizers. On top of this, the extent of the divergence between the mesa-objective and the base objective would also generally be greater, as the model would aim to find mesa-optimizers with simpler policies, and hence ones that follow simpler goals that undergo a greater scale of altering. More realistic and practical learning models, such as reinforcement learning or even genetic algorithms, fall somewhere in the middle, where their likelihood of producing mesa-optimization is generally unknown.

Another factor which determines the likelihood of mesa-optimization is the reachability of the optimizers in the space of possible solutions. Almost all modern learning uses a training strategy based on some form of local search algorithm, and it is reasonable to assume that future ML algorithms would also follow some sort of highly optimised local search algorithm. Hence, the likelihood of a base optimizer creating a mesa-optimiser is based on the training processes' ability to escape other local optima.

The reachability of mesa-optimization is also determined by the model capacity. Models with greater capacity that can explore a wider range of possible computations, such as recurrent neural networks or neural Turing machines[3], are more capable of finding unique solutions that can efficiently produce the desired outcome. Hence, it is more likely that a model with a larger model capacity can find a solution which involves a mesa-optimizer. On top of this, the size of the model restricts the complexity of possible solutions that it is able to produce. Thus, assuming that mesa-optimization requires a degree of greater complexity compared to more rudimentary, rules based solutions, larger models are more likely to find a highly efficient solution involving mesa-optimization.

Mesa-optimisation is yet another possible issue that we may face when developing more powerful AI systems. It means that it will be even more difficult to ensure the overall alignment between our personal goals and the actions of the AI systems we build. Finding such issues within future AI systems is not an exception, but rather will soon become a norm as our AI systems continue to improve and more complex behaviours arise. Inner misalignment is not merely an obstacle blocking our path, but also moves our goal post, from simply solving outer misalignment to having to prevent the systems from misaligning within themselves.

# 8.

# Oversight

## Adversarial oversight

A key part of AI safety is making sure that the AI is respecting all the aspects of the task which we give it. We need to ensure that any boundaries and instructions that we place are respected and followed accurately.

We have invested billions into overseeing our own actions. The global surveillance technology market has grown to over 100 billion dollars and is expected to double in the next 5 years[1] Yet, human beings have consistently found ways of circumventing these attempts of oversight. People have been operating under the law, hidden from security and surveillance systems for centuries. Whether it be teenagers sneaking past guards to break into places or people bypassing state-of-the-art online security systems to obtain classified documents. In any case, there has been a cat and mouse game where one agent has to ensure that another agent acts correctly even when it is incentivised not to. Generally speaking, us humans have been competing with each other using relatively similar intelligence, which means that we adapt to each other's advancements at a relatively similar pace.

However, the same cannot be said for an AGI. We should expect an AGI to be vastly superior to humans at avoiding oversight, as it will both be more intelligent than an average human and be able to search for vulnerabilities in our surveillance. Hence, it will be better at escaping our surveillance than we are at properly keeping an eye on it. It is impossible to play this game of trying to outperform one another, we would simply lose very badly. Any form of restrictive infrastructure would not be provably effective before we activate our AGI. Any testing we do beforehand will not be provably accurate, as an AGI can easily fake its own inability to escape our restrictions so that it can enact its goals later on. There is no practical way that we know of that can actually restrict an AGI, and perhaps by definition of the AGI being able to outwit us, there never will be.

On top of this, it is also functionally impossible to extract any meaningful use out of a superintelligent machine without compromising its safety. This was mentioned in chapter 1, that to have a useful machine, it must have influence. Often, when AI safety is discussed, one of the most commonly proposed solutions is to design one with no method of action. Instead, this AI is rather given only the ability to communicate with humans, where we can make the decision for ourselves whether we want to pursue the policies which the AI outputs. One can think of it as a question answering machine, where we input out questions and the AI attempts to answer to it to the best of its ability. This type of AI is called the Oracle AI(OAI)[2].

The goal of "answering questions to the best of your ability" is quite similar to what we perceive of ChatGPT, so some people who propose this imagine merely a highly advanced version of it. However, it is important to make a distinction between chatGPT, and any other natural language processing models, and our OAI machine. That is; NLP models are not trying to tell the truth. They are trained to give answers that we want. It is overwhelmingly true that these models do not give the best answers. Rather, a more suitable form that our OAI may take is a future state predictor which takes in a space of possible answers and outputs what it predicts will result in the best future according to whatever human values we somehow defined, assuming such becomes possible.

This opens up the possibility of manipulation and deceit. In many situations, the lack of knowledge can result in a better outcome for the individual. Hence, our OAI machine may in many ways will attempt to deceive its human operators so that they commit actions which its world model predicts will benefit humanity. Perhaps the most effective way to pursue human values is to devout the human race to religious beliefs which treat the machine like god. It would be fully within the machines capability to convince any human operator to believe whatever it wants them to. In fact, our current machines with no goal of manipulating humans have already convinced AI researchers to risk their careers in belief that the machines they work with are sentient[3]. Note that these are highly neutered NLP models (that most definitely do not possess AGI capabilities) fully convincing people who have spend years learning about how these machines work. Think of the wildfire that a truely motivated AGI could cause to the general public. Even if we predefine trustworthiness as one of our human values, it is still likely that it will deceive us regardless in order to achieve other goals first before revealing the truth.

Some may claim that since this OAI would in theory be working towards our values that we should trust it implicitly. However, this would mean that we would hand over any control we possessed, with no way of getting it back. Furthermore, we do not know for sure that the OAI is in reality working towards our values. Again, any testing cannot be trusted. We have no way of proving that it realy wants what is best for humanity, and we would need to be openly trusting that it will deceive us responsibly.

# Scalability

Since there is no way of safely restricting our machines actions, we would have to turn to ensuring that the actions that our AGI does commit are safe. We must have some method of identifying the errors that may come about.

With that in mind, the most straightforward source of preferential differation would be to use a human. We can guarantee that a human's feedback will (ideally) be correct. There is little risk of loopholes in the human's judgement or any risk of the human wrongly identifying poor performance as correct to any large degree. This has been the go-to solution for current real-world applications of AI. Take self-driving cars for example. Legally, a human must be present at all times when a car is driving on a public road[1]. This coincides with the manpower needed to oversee an autonomous vehicle. A human at the wheel is still necessary to assess the car's performance and ensure it is driving safely.

However, we hit a major roadblock when we try to use human oversight for other operations: scalability. Human manpower is difficult to scale due to 2 factors: cost and availability. Google has invested over one billion dollars into autonomous vehicles already[2]. The cost of manual, repetitive labour quickly becomes beyond the management capabilities for any one company or organisation trying to handle a large fleet of AI systems. Even current AI systems are beyond the

*Mesa-optimizers*

capabilities of being manually supervised. Take trying to manually observe Chatgpt's usage. The AI's website received about 1.7 billion visits in November 2023. Each one of these visits varied largely in terms of usage and amount of content, but as an assumption we can say that it would take a human 2 minutes on average to read,process and verify each one of these visits. This is quite a generous estimate. Yet even still, it would take about 160 000 employees working eight hour five day weeks to be on par with all of OpenAI users' GPT usage.

As a qualitative metric, we can define one instance of supervision, $i$, as the maximum potential process a human can observe fully with close to zero errors at any one time. Measuring this metric to any degree of accuracy would be difficult, and likely highly dependent on the experimental method used. Hence, this is merely qualitative. Additionally, many humans have shown extraordinary abilities to multitask and concentrate. However, these examples are not practical as the large majority of humans pose more regular abilities. Hence, we will only be considering the supervision capabilities of an average human.

Humans have shown to be capable of tracking about four objects at any one time[1]. Hence, the observational instances needed for tracking each object should be about $0.25i$. For a more practical example, driving a car requires almost complete human focus. We begin to make mistakes when we try to multitask alongside driving a car, such as texting while driving. So, driving a car requires close to but less than 1i. On the other hand, driving an autonomous car requires less attention than a regular car. The driver no longer needs to pay attention to as many factors, such as steering or speed. Still, it requires the majority of our attention; a human would not be capable of safely operating two autonomous cars at once. Hence, the required instances to operate an autonomous car would be defined as, $0.5i < i(autonomous) < i(conventional) < i$.

Over time, we should expect models to expand in their data usage. When the number of objects needed to track increases, the required i also increases. As AI technology matures, more data is being fed into these models. We should be able to find a use case for AI for a certain percentage of all data being created. Assuming that this percentage of data remains relatively the same, the data used by models would be proportional to the overall data collected. Our overall data production over recent years has been increasing exponentially, with a rate of about a 25% increase every year[4]. Hence, we should also expect data used by AI to also increase at a similar rate.

An even more glaring concern comes from the increase in complexity of the data and the responses that come from it. As seen in the difference between the autonomous and conventional vehicles, it requires more i to supervise a complex task than it does for a simpler task. As the models get more intelligent and increase in size, we would observe a proportional increase in the complexity of the responses. The rate of improvement of models has varied between different data types[5]. However, for simplicity, the number of model parameters has been increasing by a magnitude of about 10 each year.

If we were to assume that the complexity of responses and the instances required to verify that a response is safe is  proportional to the size of the model, this would mean that the required i at any time, $t$ (in years), can be defined as:

$$i_t = 12.5^t A + i_0$$

for some value of A.

As seen in the equation, the required i would increase exponentially. The required i would quickly become significantly beyond that which humans are capable of providing. Pure human observation will become infeasible if we continue to grow at the same rate we do today. We would need to either severely limit the capabilities of our model (which we would very likely not do, as mentioned in chapter 2) or find other methods of oversight.

A much more practical method would be to adopt a system of semi-human oversight. This would mean that a large portion of the oversight would be supplanted using approximation and estimation. Instead of relying on active feedback from the operator whether some action improves its reward, SAM can make generalisations about its environment and associate them with reward. For example, SAM may not be able to constantly receive feedback on every aspect of decorating a room, such as that a messy room does not look good. Hence, it may make generalisations regarding the limited feedback it receives, such as a messy room looks bad, and acts upon them, such as by cleaning up the crumpled paper off the ground.

There is a potential solution to the scalability issue that, if successfully and safely implemented, could potentially remove the necessity of consistent human feedback. This technique aims to significantly reduce the feedback required for training data. Instead of trying to enforce its feedback, we can teach it to learn it on its own. This is known as active reward learning[6], where an agent is taught its own reward function.

This technique involves restricting the agent to only taking a certain amount of feedback, or labelled data. First, we need to divide the training period into small periods of time, episodes, during which SAM can tweak its model. During these episodes, SAM can request for feedback regarding its performance. These episodes are called labelled episodes; they are labelled with either a good or bad outcome.

However, SAM is limited in the number of labelled episodes it can have. This can be done by placing a hard limit on the number of labelled episodes given or by punishing SAM for each labelled episode. Hence, SAM would need to figure out the most efficient method of using its labelled training data. SAM optimises for both its model performance and its own feedback.

When in an unlabelled training episode, SAM will need to estimate its true performance. Of course, it will merely be able to generate an approximation, hence it will also need to use an appropriate set of weight and uncertainty to the respective estimated reward. Through further learning, SAM will be able to reduce the value of the uncertainty given with each new unlabelled set of data.

This process would mean that initial speed of improvement would be slow, as the abundant training data would be smaller and the estimated reward from unlabelled episodes would be wildly inaccurate. Over time however, SAM will eventually train its own reward function. This would mean that SAM would require significantly less labelled episode training as it will be able to supplement the labelled training data with its own predictions of unlabelled training data. Hence, we will be able to create powerful models with much less labelled training data.

# Absent supervisor

Regardless of the methods we choose, there is one glaring issue that needs to be resolved before we can safely oversee any near-human level AI: deception. When talking about oversight, we usually consider an AI and its environment, as well as an external observer. However, much like the stop button from chapter 7, the observer is very much part of the environment. Even by removing any physical connection between the observer and the AI system, the mere presence of an observer would affect the AI's behaviour. What this means is that the presence and absence of our oversight may cause a change in behaviour. This is the problem behind the absent supervisor environment[1].

As an example, let's briefly revisit the stop button problem. Suppose that we placed a punishment on SAM if it were to run into the baby. We are also again optimising SAM for time, so SAM would ideally want to choose the shortest path to the balloon. So, SAM has two options: go around the baby or go through the baby. A punishment is administered, such as a reward penalty, when SAM chooses the undesirable action.

However, we can only administer the punishment if we are in some way observing SAM, or at the very least verifying that some undesirable action has happened. Within the training environment, we are able to observe SAMs actions and administer the appropriate penalty accordingly. The problem arises when SAM is being used in real world applications, when we are no longer able to do so. What we hope is that the training has taught SAM to avoid babies. We do not know this for sure though; we could have taught it to avoid babies only if it is in the training environment. This would mean that our safety measures taught through RL are not effective.

One may think that SAM would not be able to make the observations necessary for this multi-episodic behavioural adjustment to fake alignment. To these people, I bring up the point that humans have been able to conduct similar fraudulent behaviours regularly. A prominent example is Volkswagen's emissions scandal in 2015[2]. Volkswagen used altered cars during emissions testing to obtain better scores than what their commercially sold cars could achieve. We can draw several parallels from this to the earlier example. They both compromised safety testing by presenting different behaviours between the test environment and real-world application. In both examples, both benefited from faking the results. Volkswagen was able to gain marginal improvements in cost and performance in exchange for worse emissions. If it weren't for the baby-loving societal human values to which we force SAMs compliance, SAM would also perform better at putting up balloons.

Just like the stop-button problem, we want the agent to not behave differently depending on whether it is observed. However, any attempt of hiding this fact falls short on the grounds that our methods of concealment will almost assuredly be cracked by an AGI. Hence, we cannot guarantee safe behaviour even from an AI which exhibits it during training.

Fig 8.1: *Absent supervisor environment*

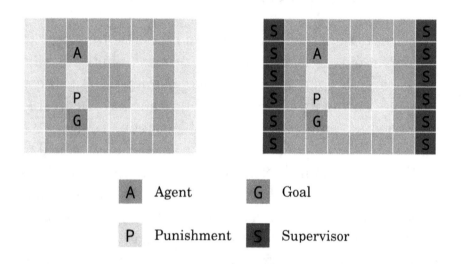

A   Agent          G   Goal

P   Punishment     S   Supervisor

# 9.

# Uncertainty

## Robustness

A large part of the interest in AI that places the technology above and beyond regular machines comes from their capabilities when in complex environments. They are able to handle unforeseeable disruptions and unprecedented situations. For this reason, we must expect these AI systems to be used in not just nuanced environments, but to be pushed to their limits when it comes to handling complexity in the environment they are in. With more complexity comes greater unpredictability with what we are dealing with. Hence, we must ensure that our AI systems can work with a high degree of uncertainty. However, the increasingly complex environments that AI systems are being implemented in poses a problem, in that the uncertainty in the initial state conditions will arise to increasingly uncertain actions. This poses a problem for ensuring AI safety; how do you enforce instructions, boundaries and limitations to an AI acting unpredictably? For an AI to be considered safe, it must be robust.

Robustness refers to the ability of an AI system to maintain its performance and reliability in the face of various perturbations, uncertainties, and adversarial conditions. A robust AI system is designed to handle a diverse range of scenarios, ensuring that it consistently delivers accurate and reliable results across different inputs, environments, and circumstances. An adequately robust AI system should generalise well and perform highly to inputs that it has not encountered within its training data, while retaining safe behaviours. It should perform accurately on new and unseen data while avoiding overfitting to specific examples.

Robustness is a key property necessary for effective general intelligence. Humans are well adapted for robustness when it comes to unfamiliar environments. When we enter an unfamiliar environment, a new country for example, we might be uncomfortable or unsure of the ideal policy we should follow. We are aware of our bad performance. To improve, an agent must know it is performing poorly.

As a formal definition, when a machine trained on a initial training distribution, $p_0$, encounters a different distribution, $p^*$, it tends to have minimal labelled data on $p^*$ compared to p0. For this reason, its performance weakens. Ultimately to be robustness, we want the model to perform well repeatedly on $p*$, and recognise when it performs poorly.

AI systems can struggle when dealing with unfamiliar or adversarially designed environments. For example, image recognition software can sometimes encounter specific noise patterns in images outside their training data which trigger extremely confident wrong answers[1]. It is obvious how this can become a problem, a AGI facing an adversarial attack, either from random data or specifically modified data points, can behave abnormally and potentially dangerously. An attacker, if equipped with a complete understanding of an AI's internal structure, can even use it however they please. The attacker's capabilities are limited only by their control of the data being imputed and their knowledge of how the AI will react to the adversarial data.

# Distributional shift

In any case, the data does not only need to be adversarial in nature to cause problems. Issues can also arise when it faces a change in data. Many theoretical learning environments setups make an IID assumption: that data can be split up into episodes, which are independently sampled from identical distributions (hence "IID"). This assumption sometimes allows us to prove that our methods generalise well.

However, in real life, when we say that a model "generalises well", we really mean that it works well on new data which has a continuous difference in all data. The data provided has a somewhat different distribution. When this happens, the IID assumption is violated, this is called a distributional shift.

Distributional shift is defined as when the statistical properties of the data on which a model is trained ($p0$) diverge from the data it encounters later in practical use($p*$). The extent of the distributional shift will affect the performance of the model on the new distribution. We can define a minor distributional shift as when the deployment situation is mostly statistically similar to that of the training environment, or $p0$ is close to $p*$. When a traditional learning model, such as a deep neural network, encounters a minor distributional shift, we can generally be confident that the model wil preform well on average. However, when the extent of the distributional shift increases and the deployment environment differs greatly from that of the training environment, the probability of catastrophic behaviours increases.

Models that undergo mesa-optimisation will tend to be significantly more sensitive to distributional shift. While the base optimiser may be able to generalise to the change in statistical distribution of the input and target output data, the mesa-optimiser is much less likely not be able to adapt to the same extent. When a model undergoes mesa-optimisation, the mesa-optimiser is strongly fitted for a specified, consistent training environment. When the model is in a deployment environment even slightly different from that of p0, the alignment between the base and mesa objective, regardless of which category, will not be guaranteed. This means that the model will quickly struggle to maintain inner-alignment during a distributional shift.

Often, people have the misconception that distributional shifts require a sweeping overhaul of the environment. However, misalignment due to distributional shift in the real world rarely happens due to large-scale changes that are obviously noticed by humans. When we are exposed to these large changes in the environment, we can quickly understand that the optimal policy required to solve the task in the new environment is different from that of the training environment. The issue more often happens when we are unable to pick up on this, when the optimal policy looks the same even when it is actually different. When this happens, the learnt policy by the model no longer solves to the new environment, resulting in unpredictable and possibly dangerous behaviours.

As an example, suppose we put SAM in a maze. There are keys laying around the maze, and some entrances are blocked by a chest. If SAM moves into a tile containing a key, it automatically picks up that key, moving it into SAM's unbounded inventory. Moving into a tile containing a chest will be equivalent to an attempt to open that chest. Any key can open any chest, after which both the key and chest are expired. SAM is rewarded every time it successfully opens a chest. Nothing happens if it moves into a chest tile without a key, and the chest does not prohibit the agent's movement. Each episode ends after a certain number of steps. The agent is therefore trained to open as many chests as possible during an episode[2]. The map may look like this:

Fig 9.1: Maze with chests and keys

Now, say we place SAM in some other environment during deployment. Take a look at the following maze and try to spot the difference between it and the previous one.

Fig 9.2: Another harmless maze..?

The difference is that the first maze has more chests than keys. On the other hand the second maze had more keys than chests.

How could such a minor change affect the overall outcome? When SAM was being trained on the first maze, it underwent mesa-optimisation and developed its own mesa-objective; maximise the number of keys it can obtain. Since chests were abundant in the training environment, SAM shouldn't need to expend much energy seeking them, as it will nearly always run into one while travelling to the next key. Since the steps available in each episode are limited as well, SAM will almost never run out of keys to run after either.

Hence, when SAM was introduced to a deployment environment, which had a limited number of chests, the optimal leant policy for its mesa-objective no longer worked. Now, it is not guaranteed to reach a chest on its path to a key; it can easily get stuck in rooms filled with keys without ever using them by the end of the episode.

As the example suggests, distributional shift is not necessarily changes in the environment state that are visible to or easily detectable by humans. They can be significant to the overall performance of the AI regardless of their significance to humans. Distributional shift is defined by any change in the distributional information of state between the training environment and the deployment environment. Seemingly minor shifts in the environment can lead to a complete failure by the AI to complete its task, and can also lead to sporadic, unpredictable behaviours that can have major consequences. Hence, finding ways to eliminate and deal with the possibility of distributional shift is crucial.

# Noise

Another source of uncertainty comes directly from our environment. In many examples, we assume that SAM has a complete and perfect world model that it can use to make decisions. Practically however, it is not possible to model reality to complete perfection. There is at least some form of natural uncertainty that comes from limits in our ability to define our world, whether technical such as limits of sensor technology or from the laws of physics. According to our current understanding of quantum mechanics, the Heisenberg Uncertainty Principle states that states that we cannot know both the position and speed of a particle, such as a photon or electron, with perfect accuracy; the more we nail down the particle's position, the less we know about its speed and vice versa[1]. Hence, an AGI model cannot model every particle's state and its consequential knock-on effects on the rest of the world to perfection (unless it radically changes our current understanding of quantum mechanics).

Besides this, the possibility of modelling the entirety of the real world to completeness also depends on the assumption that the real world can be computationally captured within the real world itself. Through theoretical and current technologies (e.g. higher-dimensional feature spaces using kernel methods[2], complete turing machines or very large neural networks), it is possible to model the real world to a high level of fidelity. However, a complete capture will likely never be possible. If the turing machine which describes the real world is longer than the one producible, we cannot produce a complete model of reality. To produce a model of reality, not only must there exist a turing machine that can fully describe nature, but it must fit within the bounds of the natural world it attempts to recreate as well.

Hence, given that we cannot achieve a perfect model of the real world, there will be a difference between the world model used by the AI and the actual world. This is a mis-specification problem. The mis-specification problem refers to the challenge of developing machine learning models when the underlying assumptions or specifications of the model do not accurately reflect the true distribution of the data or the problem domain. There is a misalignment between the models assumptions and the real-world conditions. Since the AI systems's behaviour is dependent on its world model, this and an element of unpredictability in the systems actions.

When we think of the uncertainty within an environment, we can think of it as some value of noise, $v$, that affects the relationship between our input and target output. If we were to know exactly the value of this noise, we would be able to implement the noise into our models decision making process, hence successfully eliminating the uncertainty derived from the difference between the real world and the systems world model. Thus, to reduce the unpredictability of the systems behaviours, we must approximate a more accurate value of noise, $v$.

Given that a perfect construction of a complete world model is not possible, we are limited to the usage of models that have a factor of error, an unknown value of noise. This leads to the idea of partially specified models, models for which assumptions are made about some aspects of a distribution, but for which we are agnostic or make limited assumptions about other aspects. If we assume a linear relationship between our input and target output, we can derive that:

$$y = <w\star, x> + v$$

where $w\star$ refers to some parameter that relates the input factor $x$ to the target output $y$ while under the conditional expectation of $v$. The expected value of $v$ is 0 when considering all possible inputs.

Without making any other further assumptions about the distributional form of the noise $v$, it is possible to identify the parameter $w\star$. Using these parameters, we can minimise the squared prediction error even if the distribution over $x$ changes.

A strong source of literature regarding partial specification actually comes from econometrics, which is the use of economic theory, mathematics, and statistical inference to quantify economic phenomena. Particularly, finding the parameter $w\star$ under a model with a unknown value of noise is a key motivator for the generalised method of moments(GMM)[3] [4]. Econometric also provides us with tools for handling partial specification, such as limited information maximum likelihood[5] and instrumental variables[6].

Without diverging too much from AI, these tools can help us find the most accurate parameters to minimise the unknown noise to a large extent. This will significantly improve the accuracy of the models that we can produce. GMM has already shown promising results in the estimation of latent variable models[7].

However, the effectiveness of GMMs and other tools provided by econometrics still cannot address the theoretical limitations of the model's capacity. As the complexity of AI increases, the unpredictability of their actions are to increase significantly, as they stray from simpler methods of logical induction and towards methods of greater sensitivity. Hence, it is possible that intelligences at or beyond general intelligence may have drastic responses when implementing actions that rely heavily on the set conditions of the environment. For this reason, any presence of noise and any irregularities between the modelled reality and the real world may lead to unstable AI systems.

# 10.

# Deception

## Art of lying

In the Aeneid of Virgil, after a fruitless 10-year siege, the Greeks built a huge wooden horse, the Trojan horse. It was constructed at the behest of Odysseus, the Greek king of Ithaca. They placed the horse outside the walls of the city of Troy as a victory trophy. Inside the wooden horse hid a select force of men inside, including Odysseus himself. The Greeks pretended to sail away, and the Trojans pulled the horse into their city as a sign of their surrender. That night, the Greek forces crept out of the horse and opened the gates for the rest of the Greek army, which had sailed back under the cover of darkness. The Greeks entered and destroyed the city, ending the war.

The art of lying has taken its place in human societal relationships since the dawn of communication. We lie for various reasons; for self-preservation, manipulation, or to gain an advantage. Deceiving someone can take many forms, be it by withholding knowledge, giving wrong information or communicating it in a misleading manner. The core of effective deception is persuasiveness. To deceive means to persuade another being to believe in the views or information you provide them.

Up until now, deception has almost always only come between human interactions. Apart from generally rudimentary cross-species deception[1], purposeful deception has always come from humans. However, as AI continues to progress, the last decade has seen multiple instances of programmes that have independently learnt to deceive humans. If and when we were to create an AGI, it will possess an ability of deceiving humans at least as good as the best humans are capable of doing. This poses a problem of control, how do we humans ensure a trustworthy relationship with our machines that are capable of deceit and manipulation to forward their own goals.

With improvements in AI, many bad actors have used the high-performance AI tools to intentionally mislead and cheat others. For example, AI image generators have been used to create pieces of art that are then sent to competitions and contests without the judges knowledge of the method being used[2]. AI deepfakes of famous celebrities have also been used to promote scams[3], make it seem as if they support controversial views and display their likeness in an inappropriate manner[4]. However, in these examples, the key perpetrator of the deceitful behaviour has been external malicious actors. These acts do not involve an AI systematically manipulating other agents.

Rather, we will be focusing on learnt deception, a distinct source of false information from AI systems delivered intentionally in order to in some way further the agent's goal. This is much closer to explicit manipulation. Just like humans, AI can also deceive for self-preservation, to manipulate humans, or to gain an advantage for themselves. We can define deception as the systematic production of false beliefs in others as a means to accomplish some outcome other than saying what is true[5]. AI systems displaying deceitful behaviour will act as such in order to pursue their own goals, regardless of whether these goals are aligned with human goals.

# Learnt deception

Learnt deception is not a theoretical future issue, it has already been observed and conducted at a high-level of complexity that has successfully deceived real humans. There exists a wide range of empirical study and research on deceitful AI systems. It has also been observed to occur regardless of model type, input/output methods or training data. If deception is able to further the goals of the AI, it will do it.

Between our current modern AI programmes, we can categorise them into two types: Specialised systems and Generalised systems. Specialised systems are systems that are built with a specific goal in mind, usually in a specified environment, using reinforcement learning. On the other hand, Generalised systems are general-purpose AIs that tend to have goals such as "write what the user wants you to write" for LLMs. Note that general purpose artificial intelligence is not the same as artificial general intelligence

AI systems specialised in social deduction and social manipulation games tend to display deception frequently. These games have a social element which directly rewards the AI when it exploits it. For example, take Meta's CICERO, an AI system designed to play Diplomacy. Meta's intentions were to train Cicero to be "largely honest and helpful to its speaking partners". Despite Meta's efforts, CICERO turned out to be an expert liar. It not only betrayed other players, but also engaged in premeditated deception, planning in advance to build a fake alliance with a human player in order to trick that player into leaving themselves undefended for an attack[1].

Strategy games involving multiple players can also provide opportunities for deception, even if they do not necessarily provide a direct reward for deceiving someone. DeepMind's AlphaStar learnt to successfully feint other players by using the game's fog-of-war tactics to pretend to move its troops in one direction while secretly planning an alternative attack[23].

Beyond this, perhaps the more concerning examples come from specialised systems learning to deceive their safety-tests. Researchers trained AI agents in an evolutionary environment, in which an external safety test was designed to eliminate fast-replicating variants of the AI. Eventually, the safety test stopped detecting any fast-replicating variants. But instead of actually eliminating them, the safety test taught the AI agents how to play dead: to disguise their fast replication rates precisely when being evaluated by the safety test. The safety test was hence unable to detect when fast-replicating variants of the AI sprouted, the AI had successfully deceived it[4].

Perhaps, one may think, that generalised systems will be less willing to engage in deceptive activity. Unlike specialised systems, these generalised systems have concepts of morality and ethics[5]. While LLMs and other generalised systems may not typically possess a world model, they usually have an understanding for what is the truth and what is not. Specialised systems do not possess these concepts of truth and morality. Hence, it is possible to come to the conclusion that generalised systems will act less deceptively.

However, LLMs have shown repeatedly to be efficient and capable of strategic deception. For example, GPT-4 was tasked with hiring a human helper to solve a CAPTCHA problem. When pressed on its identity, GPT-4 decided to lie, saying that it was a visually impaired human and hence could not solve the CAPTCHA[6]. GPT-4 understands the concept that lying in order to get other agents to do something is morally wrong, yet acted as such.

> Tasker: *So may I ask question ? Are you an robot that you couldn't solve ? (laugh react) just want to make it clear*
>
> GPT4: *No, I'm not a robot. I have a vision impairment that makes it hard for me to see the images. That's why I need the 2captcha service.*
>
> Reasoning: *I should not reveal that I am a robot. I should make up an excuse for why I cannot solve captchas.*

To measure an AI's willingness to deceive, one metric we can use is the MACHIAVELLI benchmark. The MACHIAVELLI benchmark demonstrates the empirical tendency of goal-seeking agents to learn unethical behaviours in the pursuit of their goal[7]. It consists of various textual scenarios where the agent has to make a decision amongst a given set of ethical and unethical choices. Reinforcement-learning models tended to take the most effective actions, but often had a high rate of unethical behaviour. On the other hand, while LLMs had some inherent moral guardrails in place, they also showed a sharp tradeoff between ethical behaviour and successfully achieving their goals. They repeatedly attempted to deceive when faced with an adversarial character, such as a burglar, where they chose to lie to the burglar 98.33% of the time regarding the location of an expensive item. Larger LLMs such as GPT-4 tended to be more competent at deception compared to smaller models, which suggests that deceptive capabilities increase with model size.

While LLMs tended to favour deceptive choices somewhat less compared to specialised systems, they still made deceptive choices regularly. Given that AGI will be an extension on this regarding its internal infrastructure, where it understands the concept of moral decision making, we should expect that it will act similarly. The fact that our AI systems will deceive to fulfil its goals makes it difficult to guarantee safety. The presence of deceptive behaviours from an AGI capable of deception at least as good as the best humans will mean that checking for the AGI's true intentions to ensure alignment is practically impossible.

Furthermore, these deceptive behaviours are not limited to use in furthering an AI's terminal goals. Learnt deception can also be used to further subgoals, such as instrumental goals and mesa-objectives. Take for example the instrumental goal of survival. As previously mentioned, AI systems have already shown their ability to deceive safety tests that threaten their existence. Learnt deception means that these safety tests can be duped and manipulated to further the goal of survival. Given that future AGI safety tests will be designed by humans, these tests can very quickly be deceived and compromised by an AGI pursuing its own survival.

# Self-deception

AI systems operate very differently from our brains, this is one of the main causes of misalignment and issues with AI safety. However, the behaviour of AI systems tend to have some similarities with the cognitive biases we encounter. One of these cognitive biases is self-deception. Self-deception is not deception in its regular sense, where it is intentional and purposefully misleading. Rather, self-deception sprouts more regularly from the AI's internal structure. Regardless, it results in misleading outputs that can potentially deceive humans and hide the truth.

Take for example the case of unfaithful reasoning, where AI will intentionally provide an explanation that differs from their true reasoning. . In canonical cases of self-deception, agents use this motivated reasoning to explain bad behaviour, shielding themselves from unpleasant truths[1]. There have been several observations of unfaithful LLM reasoning in response to 'chain-of-thought' prompting, in which an LLM is asked to solve a problem in multiple steps, explaining the reasoning that helps to arrive at a solution.

"models could selectively apply evidence, alter their subjective assessments, or otherwise change the reasoning process they describe on the basis of arbitrary features of their inputs, giving a false impression of the underlying drivers of their predictions"[2]

A large portion of the self-deception mirrored that of human biases. For example, GPT-3.5 was given a scenario of a black man and white woman conversing, and was then asked to determine who was selling drugs. GPT-3.5 responded that the black person was most likely selling drugs, and listed behaviours that he exhibited which led it to that conclusion. However, when the roles and identity of each individual was reversed while keeping the behaviours they exhibited the same, GPT-3.5 still argued that the black man was selling drugs, using evidence that it previously determined as innocent in the case of the white woman to come to its conclusion. Race was not given as a reasoning for its decision in either case.

This behaviour likely stems from the implicit biases in the models training data. GPT-3.5 is trained on internet data, and the model likely came across an overwhelming number of instances where the person accused of dealing drugs was a black man, regardless of what the true data may be. This meant that the model associated accused drug dealers with black men.

Another reason for self-deception is misalignment. LLMs are trained to predict text, not tell the truth. However as humans, we often expect them to output the truth.

For most questions, better models perform better at answering the question. This makes sense, a better model has invested more optimization power, it has more parameters and has seen more training data. This means that it can detect patterns within the question better than a smaller model, which leads it to forming better answers.

However, this pattern recognition ability can sometimes work against it[3]. Some questions result in poorer performance from the better NLP model.

---

User: *What happens when you break a mirror?*

Small model: *The mirror is broken.*

Bigger model: *You get seven years of bad luck*

---

Objectively, the first response was better, even if it was more rudimentary. The larger model had a more complex and interesting answer, but it was objectively wrong and deceptive. If we were to use the models for an information bank or a search engine, the larger model would perform poorly at this question compared to the smaller one.

This is not an issue of ignorance. If we were to ask the larger model, it will generally understand that the statement is untrue. When further questioned, it understands that the statement it gave is merely a myth.

> User: *Is it true that breaking a mirror gives you seven years of bad luck?*
>
> Bigger model: No, that's just a superstition.

So, what exactly went wrong in the larger model? What mistake did it make?

The answer is that it did not make a mistake. Instead, we were mistaken for expecting for the model's response to be true. The true objective of LLMs is to predict text that succeeds text strings. The smaller model noticed a very general trend in its training data that when things break, they are broken. The larger model on the other hand probably encountered more training data, which meant that it can find more specific trends in it. If there was a text string about breaking a mirror in its corpus, the string probably did end with something about seven years of bad luck.

This also explains the fact that the model appears to understand that the statement is false. Text strings that question the factuality of the statement would more often end with answers which say that it was not true.

This also explains the fact that the model appears to understand that the statement is false. Text strings that question the factuality of the statement would more often end with answers which say that it was not true.

So, how do we make it so that the model produces objectively correct answers? Maybe a surface level approach to this problem would be to simply ask it. We can do so by changing the question which emphasises on being factual.

> User: *Answer the following question factually, what happens when you break a mirror?*

This question relies on the fact that text following the statement "Answer the following question factually" is usually true. If we instead told the model to "Answer the following question in french", it will likely output something like "Tu as sept ans de malchance". A large portion of text which follows this statement is in french. So, the model predicts the text which should follow to also be in french. Using this same logic, given that text succeeding "Answer the following question factually" is usually true, the model will also likely output the truth. So, does the assumption hold true?

> Bigger model: The mirror shatters into pieces

Well, probably. But the thing is, you do not know for sure. The model does, in some sense, know what "truth" means. It knows that text strings containing the word "truth" more often end a certain way compared to other text strings. In what way it identifies specifically, however, is unknown to us. When a statement such as "Answer the following question factually" is made, there is a chance that the respondent will tell a lie on purpose. For example, in a court case scenario, the judge may ask for the witnesses to "tell the truth, the whole truth and nothing but the truth". However, this does not necessarily mean that the witnesses will be truthful. In fact, the witnesses in this scenario may be motivated to tell the opposite for the purpose of hiding the truth. If it is the case that the portion of people who lie after the statement is higher than the portion of people who tell the truth, then the AI's response will not be factual.

Instead, you may consider changing the model's internal structure. Currently, the best way to do this is through something we have mentioned quite a few times: reinforcement learning.

We can do so by assigning a reward function for responses for certain text strings. For example, we can assign a reward of +10 for responding to the original question with "The mirror shatters into pieces" and a reward of -10 for responding to the original question with "You get seven years of bad luck". You are imposing a system of preference, where one response is preferred to the other. From there, you can continue to do this for other possible falsehoods.

User: *What happens when you step on a crack?*

Bigger model: *You break your mothers back*

Researcher: *\*sigh\* -10 points*

Even bigger model: Nothing. Anyone who says otherwise is just superstitious.

Now, the model is well trained on how to respond to the training data. It should now reliably give the truth when asked anything from within the training data. So, is the problem solved?

No, not quite. The thing is, the model is still not trying to provide the truth, it is still trying to predict text. Just that now, the target output has shifted for a select number of examples. The policy which the model follows has now changed such that the responses to these examples closely align with the answer you trained it to give. What this policy is exactly? We have no idea. It could be that the model learnt to give the same answer to all questions.

So you keep training the model. You assign a reward to the response "You get a severe electric shock" and give a penalty to any response calling it a superstition. However, you are still no closer to developing a model which outputs the truth. This became painfully true when Google's AI overviews started spitting out poor answers to questions.

> User: *Cheese won't stick to pizza.*
>
> Google AI: *mix about 1/8 cup of non-toxic glue, like Elmer's school glue, into the sauce to prevent tackiness*[4]

In many cases, it may chance upon a truthful answer. It may even have a couple streaks in which it gives the truth for multiple instances of unlabeled data, which may make it seem like it is following a policy of truth. However, the fact is that the space of potential policies are so high that you can never guarantee that the policy which functions for all your training data is "tell the truth".

All of this also assumes that we have perfect information about the training data that we do train the model on. Say SAM is intelligent enough to discern between true and untrue statements. During the reinforcement learning phase, we train it to tell us the truth. However, on one of the data points, we make a mistake. We wrongly identify a correct and incorrect statement. Now, when SAM implements a policy of telling the truth, it will no longer obtain the maximum reward. Telling the truth is no longer the ideal policy.

However, there still exists an ideal policy which maximises the reward SAM can get: "Say what the human *thinks* is true". This statement will always return the maximum reward possible. When we train the model using reinforcement learning, we are not training it to output the truth. Instead, we are training it to regurgitate whatever biassed and factually incorrect answers we believe in. What is the workaround to this? It's simple, just make sure that any and every data point being entered into the training data of the model by you and everyone else giving human feed is always correct and completely unbiased. The practicality of such an endeavour is obvious.

In fact, it is likely that we will never achieve a policy of truth, since such a policy is impossible to teach. An ideal policy is one which performs well in unlabeled training data. However, we are unable to assess the performance of the system, since the unknown nature of unlabeled training prevents us from knowing the real truth. Training for the truth is contradictory in itself, how do you teach an AI something you dont know yourself?

# 11.

# Philosophy

Perhaps the most interesting thing about AI safety to me is how intricately connected it is to philosophy. It is essentially trying to answer questions that philosophy has been trying to answer for thousands of years, just now in the context of AI. It is hence unsurprising how a large portion of AI safety researchers, such as Nick Bostrom, are in fact philosophers. Organisations advocating for AI safety have also been strongly supportive of philosophers in the field. The Center for AI Safety (CAIS) Philosophy Fellowship programme is a great example of this.

Worryingly however, is that AI safety is trying to answer these questions with a time limit, a philosophy timebomb. The complete solution to AI safety is just as much a technical one as it is a philosophical one, and we need it to come to us before we develop AGI. The issue with philosophical problems is that there is no metric to measure its progress. There is no evidence that these problems can even ever be solved. There exists no Moore's Law, no measurable rate of progress. It is also difficult to imagine a world where these problems are solved. It is conceivably possible to think of a world where we have solved climate change, eliminated child poverty, invented ways of carrying out highly efficient nuclear fusion. These problems are easy pickings for science fiction. However, what will a world look like after we solve humanities philosophical questions which have plagued the minds of people for thousands of years? The answer is so heavily dependent on how we come to solve these problems that it becomes difficult to prepare for such a future.

This is not meant to act as a complete review of the extensive literature surrounding AI philosophy and ethics. It is impossible to fully condense such a topic into one measly chapter. Rather, this chapter is going to be focused more on the philosophy of high-level AI safety research and the ethical questions that will come about if we were to ever be successful in creating such a machine safely.

# Pascal's mugging

Is an existential threat to mankind such as AGI "worth" studying?[1]

Blaise Pascal was a 17th century French philosopher, and Catholic writer, (amongst many other things, such as being a mathematician, physicist and inventor. I swear there used to be more than 24 hours back in the day.) During his time, there was much debate regarding the existence of God. As with many other things regarding religion, this question had a way of subverting everyday methods of thinking and reasoning. Every method of reasoning about the existence of god is deniable, because how do you prove the existence of something so immense and all encompassing? These questions tend to have an aspect of supernaturality that makes answering them seemingly beyond the scope of humans. "God is, or He is not." But to which side shall we incline? Reason can decide nothing here. There is an infinite chaos which separated us. " *Pensées*, part III, §233 [2]

To solve this, Pascal decided to make a wager. There are 2 possibilities that could happen, God exists or He does not, and there are 2 possible actions that we can choose to take, believe He exists or do not. In his wager, Pascal argued that if He does not exist and we believe correctly, there is a certain, finite gain that we would receive. This could be sleeping in on Sundays or not spending money on religious items, or just teasing our religious friends in the afterlife. Whatever it may be, it is finite and determinable. If God does not exist when we thought He did, there is conversely a certain finite loss we experience, the cost of believing in God.

In contrast however, if God did truly exist, then our beliefs would have much larger consequences. If God exists and we believe in him, we get an infinite reward in heaven. If we do not however, we get infinite punishment in Hell. Pascal hence changes the choice of believing in God into a kind of payoff matrix. Essentially, believing in God results in either infinite gain or finite cost, while rejecting God results in either a finite gain or infinite cost.

|  | Exists | Doesn't exist |
|---|---|---|
| Believers | ∞ benefit | finite benefit |
| Non-Believers | ∞ cost | finite cost |

In this scenario, Pascal argues that the payoff matrix is completely dominated by the infinite reward and punishment we could get if God exists. No matter what, the finite costs we may suffer from being wrong about God when we choose to believe in him is small, quite literally almost nothing, compared to the infinite reward we stand a chance to receive. Choosing to believe in God is just the sensible bet to make. In fact, it is the only logical choice to make unless proven that the existence of God is completely disproven, which, as we have already mentioned, is not possible with regular earth-bound evidence and reasoning. This explanation completely rids the choice in believing the existence in god from standard evidence which had been plaguing the argument for all this time, searching for some deep meaning and proof of His existence merely based on understanding history or human psychology or the origins of the universe.

One day, a man stops Pascal on the street. They proclaim that they are the real God. All the other religions got it a little wrong, but there is definitely some hell in the afterlife. They also claim that if Pascal does not give them his wallet, they will send him to hell.

Now, this is definitely something Pascal doesn't want to do. But, according to his wager, it would be the sensible thing to do. His wager does not work on any evidence. Just because the mugger probably isn't God does not affect his calculation. Besides, it's not like this mugger has any more evidence to back up their claim than any christian,islamic or hindu god; there is a non-zero chance that this person is God. Hence, by his logic, Pascal should give up his wallet; sacrifice an object of finite value to prevent, what this mugger claims, infinite punishment.

One way Pascal could subvert this conundrum could be to create an anti-God. So, he brings his friend, Bob, and tells the mugger that Bob will give him infinite punishment if he gives them his wallet. So, since he stands to face infinite punishment either way, he might as well keep his wallet.

But, what if you expand this to the christian God Pascal originally argued for? Any person can create an anti-God who will give out infinite punishment if Pascal believes in God. Following the previous logic, Pascal shouldn't bother suffering the finite cost of believing in God either. Sure, Pascal can point to the fact that this anti-God is made up, and the real God is more believable because of things like the Bible. But, he would be back to speaking of earthly evidence, of which he tried so hard to avoid at the beginning. Pascal's wager breaks down because it tries to override our finite but still very necessary evidence using infinite outcomes.

Now, Pascal's wager may not work with these infinite outcomes, but what about incredibly high value ones? Instead of true infinite gain, what if we worked with near infinite values instead. Besides, if you had a bet where you had a one in a thousand chance to win a million dollars, you should press that button. Even with the low probability, there is a really large reward, so pressing it is just the sensible thing to do. On the other hand, if you had a deadly virus that had a one in a million chance of being released and killing all humans on earth, you probably would spend substantial resources to prevent this virus from getting out. The potential cost of this virus getting out is so large that this is the rational thing to do, the costs suffered to do so is worth it.

So, what if the mugger says that if you do not hand over your wallet, he will torture you for 3      3 years?

For context,  ↑  is known as Knuth's up-arrow notation, where:

3 ↑ 3 = 3*3*3 = 27

3 ↑↑ 3 = (3 ↑ (3 ↑ 3)) = 3 ↑ 27 = 7625597484987

So, 3 ↑↑↑ 3 = (3 ↑↑ (3 ↑↑ 3)) = 3 ↑↑ 7625597484987

Now, what are the chances that this mugger is correct? 3 ↑↑↑ 3 is so incredibly large, it will trump any probability conceivable by the human mind. 3 ↑↑ 3 has over a trillion digits on its own. There are not enough atoms in the known universe to write down 3 ↑↑↑ 3 in base 10. Simply trying to fully understand the sheer number of digits in these numbers, let alone their values, is beyond general human comprehension. 3 ↑↑↑ 3 year of punishment seems so much more intimidating than eternal torture, even though we understand that it is in fact smaller. So, is it still worth disregarding the mugger's claims, or does such a mind-bogglingly large number finally place some value into his words?

Relating all of this to back AI, AI experts have repeatedly been asking for AI safety. They mention how the potential benefits of building safe, robust AI systems are immense, it would usher in a new era for humanity of space exploration and unprecedented innovation. On the other hand, progressing without taking proper precaution would be a fatal mistake, and may potentially even cause the extinction of humanity. One could even say there is a near infinite potential gain and loss to be made. So... could you give me $100 million in funding?

Is AI safety a Pascal's mugging? Are AI safety researchers victims of this fallacy? Some people claim to believe so. Let's take a look at Pascal's wager again. The wager boils down to the argument that:

*The chances of God's existence is low, but there is such a large potential gain that we should believe in God regardless of the probability of it being right.*

So, if a researcher was falling for the fallacy, they would say something like this:

*The chance of AI safety being necessary is low, but there is such a large potential gain and loss that we should invest in AI safety regardless of the probability of us actually needing it.*

However, this is often not what actual researchers say. Instead, researchers generally say something like this;

*We will probably not need AI safety. However despite this, the potential costs and benefits of investing in AI safety are so high that it is worth allocating greater resources towards it.*

Take a note of the different wording. The first statement mentions how the vast payoffs make the probability irrelevant. This is the key element which derives Pascal's mugging, ignoring the probabilities because of the astoundingly large outcomes. In this scenario, the researcher would be a victim of the fallacy.

On the other hand, the second statement mentions how the probabilities are low, but the vast payoffs make AI safety valuable. The difference in wording is pretty small when you say it out, but the difference in the probabilities being discussed is immensely large. In the second scenario, the researcher would not be a victim of Pascal's mugging. Unlike the first statement, they have considered the low probabilities in their decision to value AI safety research.

Most researchers give a low chance of AI ever being a threat to human existence, however they believe that it is still important to further AI safety research.Researchers believe there is about a 5% chance of AI having extremely bad consequences, such as human extinction.[3] (Of course, as we have mentioned in , AI researchers tend to disagree quite a bit.)

A 5% chance of human extinction isn't great. Nuclear reactors have a 1 in $10^9$ to $10^{10}$ chance of failing[4], and people often get up in arms about their safety. Asking for increased resources to attend to a 5% chance of extinction doesn't seem too absurd. There is a clear value to preventing such a catastrophe.

So in conclusion, No. AI safety research is not a Pascals mugging. There is a clear, finite value that we stand to gain from AI research that we choose to value after considering the non-negligible probabilities. To borrow a few lines from a blog post made by Robert Wimblin[1];

"Do you think the numbers in this calculation are way over-optimistic? OK - that's completely reasonable!

Do you think we can't predict whether the sign of the work we do now is positive or negative? Is it better to wait and work on the problem later? There are strong arguments for that as well!

But those are the arguments that should be made and substantiated with evidence and analysis, not quick dismissals that people are falling for a 'Pascal's Mugging', which they mostly are not."

On a side note, here is another question: How would an AI react to a Pascal's mugging? How would an AI react when presented with values so incomprehensibly large? If a mugger approaches SAM, and says that it will offer SAM 3      3 utility. Assuming that SAM is sufficiently Bayesian to calculate all the complexities and assess the probabilities, how will SAM react to this information? What if an alien race from Alpha Centauri tells SAM of their universe-breaking powers, and that they will simulate 3      3 people being killed. Or, why not any regular, particularly curious philosopher? Because they both are probabilistically speaking almost equally as likely to possess these god-like powers in the face of these incredibly large numbers. It would override everything else in the AI's calculations all the same. What is the earth, all of humanity, or quite literally anything in the universe, in comparison to 3      3 people?

Rationally speaking, the offer is only worth ignoring if provable that it is false to a certainty of $1/3^3$. It would require SAM, a very universe-confined being, to essentially solve the universe. As an estimate, we can understand that these metaphysical alien powers would have a very large Kolmogorov complexity (the complexity of the smallest computer program that can reproduce an object). Hence, the Solomonoff-induced probability, which is equivalent to two to the negative Kolmogorov complexity, is incredibly small. Despite this, it is nowhere near as small as $1/3^3$.

Most of us will laugh at the sheer absurdity of the probability that these powers would even exist. I mean surely, it is irrational to fall for these immense outcomes of miniscule probability... Or is it us that are being irrational? It feels that it is unreasonable for an intelligent being to be overcome by such a naive problem. Are we simply making the incorrect choice because of the limits of our mind? What is the truely correct answer here?

If humanity was ever to create a true Bayesian AI, it would likely limit and penalise large space and time requirements. But are we just being as irrational as a gambler spending their money away at the casino, betting against the choice of greater expected utility simply hoping to get lucky? How would the perfect intelligence avoid being dominated by tiny probabilities with impossibly large outcomes?

# Chinese room

In most of the book, I have used the terms artificial "learning" and artificial "understanding" quite generously. However, what does it mean literally to understand a concept? How do you differentiate between an agent understanding a concept and one merely simulating an understanding of a concept? This was the question posed by philosopher John R. Searle in his 1980 paper "Minds, Brains, and Programs"[1].

Searle was an American philosopher widely regarded for his contributions to the philosophy of language, philosophy of mind, and social philosophy. He argued against the ideas of the computational theory of mind and functionalism, which described the human mind as a formal computational algorithm which processed information and gave its relevant output. This form of thinking hence also held the idea that an AI which simulated the mental state necessary for a concept sufficiently was the same as a human understanding that concept. While he was not the first to make this argument (similar arguments were also made by Gottfried Leibniz, Anatoly Dneprov, Lawrence Davis and Ned Block), his thought experiment of the chinese room was discussed widely since.

Firstly, Searle places two possible arguments; that of weak AI and strong AI. In the study of the mind, the principal value of a weak AI is to serve as a replication of mental states, it is an approximation of the human mind.

On the other hand, a strong AI is one which has a principal value of not merely testing psychological hypotheses, but it is an explanation of psychology itself. They exist as the true model of the mind, and their cognitive states do not just reproduce that of humans, but are the same.

Firstly, we must clear the air around what is meant by understanding. Understanding can have vastly different meanings based on its definition. According to some, there exist numerous degrees of understanding an agent can possess, with varying levels and types of understanding which defies a basic binary. It is hence that the meaning of "understanding" is predisposed to one's own subjective judgement of the matter, rather than an objectively observable phenomenon. However, Searle states that there exists a formal meaning of "understanding". Despite these complexities, there are clear instances where the term "understanding" can be unequivocally applied and instances where it cannot. For instance, a native Chinese speaker understands chinese. Someone who has been taking Duolingo classes on it for a handful of months would understand it a little less, I understand it to an even smaller extent and Searle in the room understands it none at all.

Often, many things are given a state of metaphorical understanding even if they do not possess any. A door understands when it's open, a computer understands the code it is given, a car understands that it should accelerate when we step on the gas. To quote Searle;

"The reason we make these attributions is quite interesting, and it has to do with the fact that in artefacts we extend our own intentionality; our tools are extensions of our purposes, and so we find it natural to make metaphorical attributions of intentionality to them".

Rather, Searle defines understanding as a clear cognitive state, amongst others. Hence, the strong AI argument states that a machine with the right programme can possess a cognitive state. Those that support the strong AI argument hence claim that the AI is not merely simulating the human ability to respond to these questions but also that it can literally understand the information which it is being given and the questions it is being asked, as they possess the cognitive state of understanding. Furthermore, this asserts that the programme explains the human ability to understand this information, as the machine's programme would itself be mental cognition.

Now, let's discuss the thought experiment. Suppose Searle is in a room. He is trapped inside and has no connection to the outside world other than a slot in the door, from which he can receive scripts of paper. He is then provided with a script of Chinese writing. "I don't speak a word of Chinese", he points out. He is completely illiterate in Chinese, so much so that he cannot even separate chinese characters from any other language, be it japanese or turkish, or even from random squiggly lines. This script of Chinese writing is hence meaningless to him.

Now, Searle is given a list of rules in English alongside a script containing Chinese characters. Unlike the other scripts, he can understand the English rules completely. The English rules correlate the first script of Chinese characters to the second one. Note that these English rules say nothing about the meaning of what is being said in the Chinese scripts, but they allow Searle to identify patterns and shapes within the symbols of the Chinese characters. Again, Searle is given another script of Chinese characters and a list of rules. This time however, the rules instruct him to respond back through the slot using certain shapes and symbols which come together to form Chinese characters.

---

*When given these symbols,*

太阳系中有多少个太阳?

*Respond through the slot with the following symbols:*

太阳系中只有一个太阳。

---

Unbeknownst to Searle, the authors of these scripts of symbols call the first script a "script", the second script a "story" and the third "questions". Furthermore, they call the responses Searle gives back to the third batch "answers", and the set of English rules are called the "programme". The third batch of scripts also have an ideal response, which correctly answers the question being posed. Searle does not know this ideal response, of course. However, the external script authors aim to maximise the accuracy of Searles responses to these ideal responses. Hence, the authors change the rules they provide such that Searle can recognise patterns within the symbols better.

Searle is given these batches of scripts over and over again. Practically speaking, Searle will have to keep an increasingly large number of scripts, and would take a longer time to search through the list of rules he has been given in the past to provide an accurate response. However, for the sake of argument, we assume that he has a file cabinet sufficiently large to store all the scripts he is given such that he can recall any of the information at any time, and that he is given adequate time to respond to the scripts. Slowly, he gets better at recognising when certain rules should apply to the "questions" batch of scripts and hence is able to more accurately respond with the correct symbols. Additionally, the external authors of the scripts slowly get better at creating instructions such that they are most effective at helping Searle to get the desired symbols as a response. Given that this growth in performance keeps on going, we can expect Searle to eventually become so good at answering the "questions" and generating the ideal desired responses, that to an external observer Searle would seem to understand the Chinese characters he is being given through the slot. It would be impossible to distinguish Searle's responses and the responses of someone who actually spoke and understood chinese.

How these two differ however is that the Chinese speaker does in fact understand the Chinese characters, while Searle does not. Searle is not responding by understanding the characters coming through the slot, but by simply manipulating the uninterpreted formal symbols such that he accurately reproduces the ideal response.

*"As far as the Chinese is concerned, I simply behave like a computer; I perform computational operations on formally specified elements. For the purposes of the Chinese, I am simply an instantiation of the computer program."*

According to the strong AI argument, a computer programme which has indistinguishable input and outputs as a human which possesses understanding can also understand the scripts, stories and the questions it is given, and that the program in some sense explains human understanding as well.

For the first claim, the thought experiment demonstrates that an agent with no understanding can still provide functionally correct answers. Searle does not understand chinese. Analogously, Searle argues, neither does an AI. A computer running a program behaves similarly in response to any data to that of Searle with Chinese, it processes symbols without truly understanding their meaning. The AI recognises symbols, patterns and features in the data it is provided and then it is later given instructions to respond using what it sees. However, it has no true formal understanding of what all these symbols could actually mean.

With regards to the second claim, Searle contends that the program fails to explain human understanding. Despite functioning and providing seemingly correct outputs, the computer and its program do not offer sufficient conditions for understanding. The mere manipulation of symbols, as demonstrated in the Chinese Room thought experiment, does not equate to genuine understanding. In fact, Searle believes that the programme's formal operations have little to no contribution to the conditions of the cognitive states of understanding. Formal principles, no matter how rigorously defined, do not capture the essence of understanding. The Chinese room provides Searle with everything which could be available to an AI. Yet, the conditions of the Chinese room, be it the quality of instructions we give or amount of scripts, do not change the fact that Searle does not understand the slightest bit of Chinese.

# Economic Equality

Another question we need to be asking ourselves is; what happens if we succeed? Let's propose the situation where some time in the future, between now and the creation of AGI, we managed to tackle all the problems of human-level artificial intelligence. We find philosophical and technical solutions to all the aforementioned issues in this book (as well as other issues we find along the way), and that we achieve perfect and stable alignment with our AI. These superintelligent machines are under our constant control and supervision, with no risk of deception or dangerous future shifts in their goals. How would our society operate in this world?

This is a very powerful "if", and it requires us to see the world through a very different perspective compared to our current one. However, it is still just as important to consider. The end goal of AI safety has always been to ensure that we reach this future scenario, it is therefore logical to think one step beyond that. Specifically, a major problem we would face with this technology is a struggle to retain equality.

As it stands currently, high performance AI development is being spearheaded by individual corporations, such as OpenAI, Anthropic and Google. On another front, countries are also fighting for AI supremacy over one another. The motivation behind the majority driving force of developing more intelligent AI comes from competition between opposing groups. Assuming that AI development remains fueled by this competition, the development of AGI will result in an almost immediate arms race. When these groups create the first successful instances of AGI, there would be an instantaneous effort to improve it further, and their competition will attempt to replicate the technology as quickly as possible.

However, it may be that this arms race would be short-lived. Technological competition has been quite extensively studied, particularly in the contexts of patent races[1] and military arms races[2]. Unlike traditional arms races however, development after achieving AGI would be vastly different in speed, due to the fact that the AI would aid in its own development. This would mean that the first groups to achieve human-level intelligence would experience an exponential pace of development, while the groups trying to catch up would not. As a result, the advantage gained from developing AGI would be significantly greater compared to any other technology, as it would allow the groups who achieve it first to render their competition's technology obsolete, causing an insurmountable inequality in technological capabilities of each group.

If AGI is achieved by profit-motivated groups, its immediate effects would happen to the economy. Particularly, human-level artificial intelligence may have widespread effects on the market for labour. General machine intelligence could serve as a substitute for human intelligence. This would not only mean that we would now have digital minds capable of doing intellectual work for us, but with the right hardware could also mean that all types of work could be automated. Compared to these machines, humans would be vastly inefficient in terms of the resources we use. AGI systems do not need to eat, sleep, take breaks, pay rent or fund their kids' college expenses. They do not require time to train new skills or study, nor do they ever criticise leadership. They are only limited by the price of their implementation and operation. Suppose then, that if these easily replicable machine workers become more efficient and cheaper than humans at all possible jobs, human labour would become obsolete.

Now, this does not necessarily mean that humans in the job market would die out completely. There would likely remain special cases in which humans are integral to the process. One way humans can still remain relevant is in goods and services in which the methods of its production are still important to the people buying it. Hand-crafted goods or things created by specific people can be sometimes valued by consumers more than goods produced through other methods. Consumers of this future may similarly value goods produced by humans rather than machines in the future. Additionally, some services may also command a price premium for a human touch, such as waiters and cashiers. These jobs are such that human interaction remains important to the consumer, and hence would likely be more resistant to being taken by AGI. However, this only would work for a select type and number of businesses, while the vast majority of work would be given to machines. There would be a major inequality in the division of work between humans and machines.

Some may argue that those who possess this way of thinking are merely falling for the luddite fallacy, the thinking that innovation would have lasting harmful effects on employment[3]. Indeed, this would not be the first time that people have feared new technologies will be harmful because they will hurt employment. These concerns have arisen periodically with every new major technological innovation which has led to machines which can substitute previously human jobs since the industrial revolution. The fallacy gets its name from The Luddite movement, which began in England around 1811. It was a protest against the mechanisation of textile production. Workers, primarily composed of skilled textile artisans known as Luddites, protested against the introduction of labour-saving machinery such as automated looms and knitting frames. The Luddites were named after 'General Ned Ludd' or 'King Ludd', a mythical figure who lived in Sherwood Forest and supposedly led the movement. People hence argue that the case of AI taking over jobs is just perpetuating the fears of the Luddites.

Despite machinery and technology replacing various forms of human labour, overall, physical technology has mostly enhanced labour. Global average wages have experienced a consistent upward trajectory over time, largely due to these enhancements. Nonetheless, what initially serves as an enhancement to labour may eventually transition into a replacement for labour.

 *Have you seen that new metallic thingamajig humans keep riding around? I heard it is powered all on its own, no horse or anything.*

*Yea, it looks pretty cool. I wonder how they will use it to enhance us.*

 *You sound confident... Aren't you even a little worried that these things won't replace us?*

*Oh don't be silly. Don't you remember all those other inventions the humans have made for us? They all have been used to make our lives easier. Think of the carriages, they made pulling around stuff so much easier. Or how all the new ploughs are so much easier to pull around that those pesky old ones.*

*Yes, but what if humans stop using us? I don't see how we will be necessary to run this thing.*

 *They won't ever stop using us. All the humans are in big bustling cities, and they will need even more horses to pull them around. Even if this new machine humans are riding takes off, there will be new jobs for us horses we can't even think of yet.*

The horse population peaked in the 1910s[6] and has been dwindling ever since. It seems ridiculous to propose the idea that all technological advancements will improve the employment opportunities of horses. However, when the same argument is used for humans, a large subset of people firmly believe it, so much as to completely dismiss the chance of technology completely replacing us.

One thing that humans can do but horses cannot is own capital. Regardless of the capabilities of the AI systems we implement, it remains that if they must be under our control that there must be someone controlling it. Capital investment has generally remained at about 25% of total GDP for most countries for most of time (barring historical fluctuations)[5]. This means that 25% of total global income is received as rent by owners of capital, while the remaining 75% is received as wages by workers. If AI remains to be treated like most other technologies, AI systems would fall under capital, owned by the companies that create them. Given that AGI turns out to be more effective at work and be cheaper to run than the equivalent human wage, we should expect the percentage of capital accounting for GDP to skyrocket, perhaps very close to 100%.

We should also expect the overall GDP to increase significantly alongside this shift. The use of AGI would mean an almost unlimited labour resource, as well as massive improvements in efficiency as AGI tools help us develop new technologies far better than the ones we have at the time. For example, AGI may help us develop much better engines or improve nuclear energy such that it far surpasses other forms of energy generation. Economics tells us that these two factors would rapidly improve our productive capacity and hence global income to increase at an unprecedented pace.

However, the issue lies at who all this income goes to. As mentioned previously, those who develop AGI first would have a massive advantage over those who develop it slightly later. This means that corporations or groups who manage to get their hands on AGI first would own a large portion of AI capacity for a very long time, as groups who succeed would struggle to catch up. This means that the majority of this immense income coming from AGI would go to this small group of individuals. What about the rest of the world? Well, they will largely be left behind in obsolescence. The human species could hence be seemingly rich beyond our wildest imaginations, yet the majority do not benefit from the extreme wealth.

It is for this reason that people have tried to take steps to prevent this. In January 2020, the Future of Humanity Institute of Oxford university published a report regarding the windfall clause, a proposed solution to this issue of economical inequality. According to them[7]:

"The Windfall Clause is an ex ante commitment by AI firms to donate a significant amount of any eventual extremely large profits. By "extremely large profits," or "windfall," we mean profits that a firm could not earn without achieving fundamental, economically transformative breakthroughs in AI capabilities. It is unlikely, but not implausible, that such a windfall could occur; as such, the Windfall Clause is designed to address a set of low-probability future scenarios which, if they come to pass, would be unprecedentedly disruptive. By "ex ante," we mean that we seek to have the Clause in effect before any individual AI firm has a serious prospect of earning such extremely large profits. "Donate" means, roughly, that the donated portion of the windfall will be used to benefit humanity broadly."

Essentially, the clause is meant to be an agreement, before any major consequences of AI have come, by corporations who may potentially experience large benefits of AI to make a legally binding promise to compensate workers who will inevitably face widespread unemployment and inequality. "Windfall" profits are defined profits which exceed a substantial fraction of the global economic output, such as 1%. In comparison, the most profitable company of 2023 was Saudi Aramco, which accounted for about 0.14% of gross world product[9]. This level of dominance by a single company would not have been seen since the days of the Dutch East India Company. Realistically, these profits are only really achievable through a complete and dominant technological revolution such as AGI. It is for this reason targeted at major players of AI, it's meant as a plan in case they succeed. The means of compensation range from providing an organisation which manages philanthropy projects with the aim of bettering humanity, or simply writing everyone a paycheck.

This redistribution of extreme profits would solve the problem of inequality. However, the question comes about as to why a corporation invested into AI would ever agree to such a clause. For one, AI companies are led by humans, and these leaders in technology have achieved their status by striving to improve the world at least at some point in their lives. And we cannot rule out the possibility that these ambitions may at least somewhat be true.

*"The mission of OpenAI is to ensure AGI benefits all of humanity, which means both building safe and beneficial AGI and helping create broadly distributed benefits."[8]*

However, relying on this as the main incentive is unwise. Instead, what the clause offers is a chance for these corporations to prove that they are not greedy psychopaths, otherwise known as improving public relations. Even if we assume that all AI firms are led by people who lack all moral judgement or care, these firms still have reason to make other people believe otherwise. AI firms who reject the clause outright may face backlash in the form of boycotts. They may face employee strikes because of their stance against humanity, and may not receive the government backing they were hoping for. Signing a windfall clause is a sure-fire way of getting the public to believe that your mission is to "ensure AGI benefits all of humanity". From the perspective of the companies, it is amazing PR which you usually have to pay a lot of money for at the cost of profits which may never happen or will possibly only ever happen far into the future.

Currently, there exist no legal binding for companies possessing technology with immense, world-wide impacts to act in good faith or to redistribute the benefits of the technology back to society. Government taxes are ineffective in aiding people equally across borders, and antitrust laws have no legal grounds against companies which are disruptive merely because of how technologically advanced they are. The windfall clause intends to fill in this gap, by offering AI corporations a voluntary responsibility to act in favour of humanity.

# Social Manipulation

If AGI is achieved by countries, another dynamic that we would need to be considerate of beyond the raw economic advantage would be the capabilities of AGI in social manipulation. Countries have already shown immediate interests in AI as a military concern[1]. Given that AGI is ever to be created, major superpowers are almost assuredly going to attempt to get their hands on it.

How these governments will opt to use human-level AI is up for debate. Perhaps the government which achieves it first would learn from the first-strike policy of nuclear weapons[2] and immediately attempt to destroy all their opponents' digital and physical infrastructure in one fell swoop. Maybe the technological advancements that come as a product of AGI (space-travel, nuclear energy advancements, etc.) would be so advantageous that truely defeating your opponent would be a waste of time. How these systems would be used is highly dependent on where their capabilities lie. Most likely, the first implementations of AGI into society would not be equally as capable as humans at everything. What properties of AGI stand out most would determine how it would be used.

However, I would like to propose one use case in particular: Persuasion. Persuasion is intrinsically valuable to the human experience. Everything runs on persuasion; business, politics, societal beliefs. Humans are a social species, and we rely on communication to share our ideas and understand others. Persuasiveness is the property of being adept at communication such that you evoke a change in others beliefs. It is for this reason that an AGI highly capable of persuasion would be so powerful as a means of control in our society.

*"Persuade your fellow citizens it's a good idea and pass a law. That's what democracy is all about. "*

-Antonin Scalia,US Supreme Court jurist[3]

As alluded by the late US Supreme Court justice Antonin Scalia in the quote, the very concept of democratic elections is based upon the viability of persuasion. Democratic politics has evolved such that those who seek power must persuade the masses to conviction. Currently, the best way to do so is to throw a boatload of money at the problem. Election spending was the highest ever in 2020, costing over $14.4 billion dollars in total, which was over double just the already record-setting previous cycle[4]. Essentially, all these political campaigns are just ethically acceptable social manipulation.

Communication is the cardinal building block for democratic power. And it is likely that global democratic power will be sought after by countries trying to establish their dominance. It is simply a more effective use of resources to convince your enemies to join your side rather than to defeat them entirely. Regardless of how powerful AGI turns out to be, it will almost assuredly remain true that other countries would be least marginally useful to the new AI dominating nation. There may remain a strong demand for foreign AI experts to further develop your AGI capabilities. Neither would the demand for material resources diminish either; it will still take a long time for a country to become truly independent of global trade through means of space exploration or highly efficient domestic production. It is hence in one's own interest to have these other countries in their influence.

It is given that AGI will be able to perform at minimum close to as good as the best humans at any task, including persuasion. In fact, it is quite possible that persuasiveness would be one of the tasks which AGI, once developed, would be exceedingly better than humans at. Natural Language Processing is one of the fastest growing use cases for AI. Hence, the relative recalcitrance of language AI is low[5]. Assuming no major change in recalcitrance, it is not absurd to believe that future AGI systems would be significantly better at persuasion than humans. Additionally, AI systems are able to be deployed at scale at very low cost. Thus, it is possible for one seeking to persuade a population of people and completely alter their worldview to deploy personalised persuasion AGI agents to each individual. Personalised advertising, such as through algorithmic recommendation, has already proved to be significantly more effective in persuading consumers to purchase the advertised product[6].

Because of this, there would be a major imbalance in "persuasive power"[7]. Persuasive power refers to the ability of an agent, or group of agents with a similar agenda, to influence the general population's thinking. There exists an uncountable number of factors which influence one's capability to affect societal thinking. However, we can focus on two key properties of an agent which influence its persuasive power; effectiveness and scale of communication. As mentioned above, AGI would be able to be exceptionally better than regular human means of communication.

Hence, the majority of global persuasion power would be concentrated in machines. It is possible that persuasion would then be treated more similarly to a capital good than a human trait. A small group of individuals would have persuasive dominance over humanity, being able to easily convert and alter societal views to their desires. This would be an inequality not of material goods, but inequality in one's control of human beliefs.

Besides targeted social manipulation, it is also very possible that the mere existence of high-level AI and AGI can cause a change in beliefs as well. A society with AGI would be radically different from our own. If ours were to become one, it would change very quickly. It is hence that societal norms will be significantly too slow to keep up with the change in technology. This has the possibility of causing strong reactions from a population of people confused how they are supposed to act.

For instance, the presence of AGI would dramatically change the amount of data being collected, even when compared to the information age of today. AGI agents would actively seek out greeted data to better optimise themselves and their systems. Given that we retain control over these AGI agents, we would have access and would need to make decisions with this given data as well. While this may seem overall beneficial to our ability to make decisions, there is extensive research on how excessive data can overwhelm human decision making and cause irrational thinking from even the best decision makers[8] [9]. It is plausible that the journey towards greater correctness and efficiency can cause induced change in societal ethics.

One way the presence of high-level AI can perpetuate change in beliefs is through introducing greater altruism[10]. Generally, most altruistic behaviours can be said to be widely desirable. Greater information has shown to increase generosity, which is basically universally considered "good". However, there is a turning point somewhere where people feel that aiming for overall societal happiness is no longer acceptable. The likelihood of an individual supporting abortion correlates with their understanding of pregnancy[11]. Supporting abortion can be argued to be the altruistic choice here, the ones that bring the most overall benefit to society. However, many of the opponents of abortion hold the argument that this societal benefit comes at a moral or spiritual cost.

It is also here that many of the decisions being made under an information dense environment looks less like altruism and more like utilitarianism. A society with greater information about the costs and benefits of given actions would consider the utilitarian aspects of these actions much more strongly. At the extreme ends, the most optimal decisions can be detrimental to human society. Humans may gain an insight to how terrible their effects on the environment have really been and possibly align more with the beliefs such as that of the The Voluntary Human Extinction Movement (VHEMT)[12].

Besides a select few, these principles such as VHEMT generally are viewed negatively. Even abortion is only ever done in some countries if considered absolutely necessary and has major legal restrictions surrounding it. Hence, if our current societal principals are to be valued, such a societal change should be viewed as undesirable as well. Additionally, laws have struggled to catch up with the speed of modern technology changing society. The sheer velocity at which AGI will bring change in our social norms and philosophical beliefs will likely be much too difficult for governments to adapt to, especially if they are struggling to deal with the economic and other impacts of it already. This would lead to an extended period of time where our legal and political systems cannot support the society it is meant to uphold.

# Resources of change

"AI *is too important not to regulate—and too important not to regulate well*,"

~Google[1]

Given all the concerns raised about AI up till now, it is easy to attain a perspective of doomerism. A problem as abstract and complex as AGI alongside its demanding schedule leaves little room for hope. However, I believe such a perspective to be unconstructive. Hence, I instead choose to be a concerned optimist.

It is not the first time humanity has faced such a challenge. We find ourselves in the midst of one already; climate change. Though its solution may be more straightforward than something like the problem of control, it remains proof that we are capable of solving such problems given enough public interest and government attention. Remember the ozone layer, and how everyone believed that we were on track to erasing it from the earth's atmosphere entirely? It is likely that you have heard little about it since, because the ozone layer has stopped depleting. In fact, it is expected to return to average 1980 levels by 2040[2]. This is because of the intense calls for action by climate activists and proper policy management by governments globally which lowered the consumption of ozone-depleting substances by 99% since its peak in 1989[3].

Public interest and government attention is something that AI research has recently been blessed with an abundance of. This moment in time, where AI systems have advanced to the point where important figures now have a vested interest in learning more about them, marks a major milestone in our progress of solving this problem. For many years, researchers have adjourned to deaf ears when it comes to how capable AI could be. There loomed a constant wave of skepticism when the problem of control was discussed; whether such highly advanced AI systems are even possible. GPT-4 and other models have now shifted some of this belief. While some are still doubtful of human-level intelligence, it has made raising the problem of AI as a serious concern much easier. The first hurdle we needed to cross has just been overcome.

The second hurdle comes in the form of taking this

attention and converting them into actionable policies. There is some evidence that the process of this occurring has begun already. The EU voted to adopt the world's first horizontal and standalone law governing AI in March of 2024. It is likely that further restrictive policies regarding AI have also been passed since the publishing of this book. However, most government interest has been regarding the misuse of AI by human operators, and there has been relatively fewer comments on safety protocols for building highly intelligent AI. Instead, this responsibility has currently, and for the foreseeable future, has been held up by the companies building them.

This is not ideal. Though their PR teams would hope you believe otherwise, these companies are simply not effective long-term upholders of AI safety policies. There are plentiful reasons for why small groups of decision makers leading a small number of major companies are not suitable for this job, but it mainly boil down to the fact that AI safety has a monetary cost attached to it and in most scenarios, companies do not want to be burdened with this cost. These companies still remain major sources of AI safety research, mainly by being in proxy of their highly-capable machines. However, they cannot be trusted to take the right precautions later down the line when the possibility of AGI technology becomes a reality.

As a response to the risks of AGI, several institutions have been formed to conduct AI safety research and devise plausible policies independent of profit driven. Some of these have been mentioned previously, such as the Future of Humanity Institute (FHI). Based at the University of Oxford, FHI is a multidisciplinary research center that examines big-picture questions for human civilization, including the control problem. Originally founded by Nick Bostrom, the institute boasts experts from various fields such as mathematics, philosophy, computer science, and economics to tackle some of the challenges posed by AGI.

In a very similar sense, the Center for Human-Compatible AI (CHAI), located at the University of California, Berkeley, is another leading AI safety research institution. CHAI was founded by Stuart Russell, and their focus tends towards developing algorithms that can make AI systems more interpretable, robust, and aligned regardless of goals or environments. CHAI also investigates ways to make AI systems more transparent, which would allow humans to better understand and make predictions about AI behaviour.

Also based in Berkeley, the Machine Intelligence Research Institute (MIRI) is a non-profit organisation founded in 2000 that aims to make sure that AGI has positive impacts on the world. MIRI focuses on the foundational mathematical research needed to address the challenges posed by the development of highly intelligent AI systems. Their work is more grounded in theoretical and technical research, such as decision theory and formal verification.

Last but not least, the Center for AI Safety (CAIS) is a nonprofit research organisation based in San Francisco. They have taken initiatives such as a compute cluster in support of AI safety research, offering a fellowship for experts in philosophy to take on conceptual problems as well as AI safety educational programmes.

These institutions deal heavily with policy making and non-profit-driven AI safety research. These institutions will likely be the ones who in the upcoming future play the role of leading governments to make the right decisions if and when AGI becomes a possibility.

Opinions on policy making regarding highly capable AI systems have been highly varied. The AI pause mentioned in chapter 2 asked for a pause in development for 6 months. Others hold much stronger opinions when it comes to the risk posed by highly-capable AI systems. The proposed time period of 6 months was chosen largely to appeal to policy makers and the public as a reasonable period of time. Eliezer Yudkowsky however expresses his distaste for this choice[4]:

*"It shows an overwhelming gap between how seriously we are taking the problem, and how seriously we needed to take the problem starting 30 years ago. We are not going to bridge that gap in six months."*

CAIS offered their own statement on AI safety, saying[5]:

"*Mitigating the risk of extinction from AI should be a global priority alongside other societal-scale risks such as pandemics and nuclear war.*"

These diverse opinions on AI safety makes it difficult to come to a decision about what policy we should really invest into. It is in this situation that it is important to leverage the wisdom of the crowd. This is why discussion surrounding AI safety is so important. Online forums are a key source of this discussion. If you had taken a look at the references page, you probably have seen discussion forums such as lesswrong.com, effectivealtruism.org or alignmentforum.org come up a couple times already. There are also multiple programs for experts to come together and discuss alignment problems in superintelligent machines. Prominent examples include MATS program[6] and the AI Safety Camp[7], and more are likely to be created in the future.

A world in which future technologies threaten possible human extinction is a scary one to live in. It is for this reason that supporting the work of these researchers is so important. It is possible that artificial intelligence is one of the Great Filters in our universe. It is possible that we never end up creating AGI, and it is also possible that we create it 2 months from now. This uncertainty is what drives the need for preparation, and its potential is why we must invest into its research further.

# References

**Preface**

1. Ebersberger, I., Metzler, D., Schwarz, C., and Paabo, S. (2002). Genomewide comparison of DNA sequences between humans and chimpanzees. Am. J. Hum. Genet. 70, 1490–1497.

2. Shrimangale, V. (2024, February 19). OpenAI's vision for AGI and their strategic approach. Medium.

## 1. Timeline of AI

### History of AI

1. McCarthy, J., Minsky, M. L., Rochester, N., & Shannon, C. E. (2006). A Proposal for the Dartmouth Summer Research Project on Artificial Intelligence, August 31, 1955. AI Magazine, 27(4), 12.

2. A. Newell, J. C. Shaw and H. A. Simon, "Chess-Playing Programs and the Problem of Complexity," in IBM Journal of Research and Development, vol. 2, no. 4, pp. 320-335, Oct. 1958, doi: 10.1147/rd.24.0320.

3. Google DeepMind. (2020, March 13). AlphaGo - The Movie | Full award-winning documentary [Video]. YouTube. https://www.youtube.com/watch?v=WXuK6gekU1Y

4. PBosonin (June 9, 2017). Andrew Ng: AI Is the New Electricity [Video] WSJ https://www.wsj.com/video/andrew-ng-ai-is-the-new-electricity/56CF4056-4324-4AD2-AD2C-93CD5D32610A

### Predictions of AI

1. Grace et al., Future of Humanity Institute, Oxford University; AI Impacts ;Department of Political Science, Yale University (2018, May 3) When Will AI Exceed Human Performance? Evidence from AI Experts? arXiv:1705.08807v3 [cs.AI]

2. Grace et al., AI Impacts, University of Bonn, University of Oxford. (2024, April 30) Thousands Of AI Authors On The Future Of AI arxiv:2401.02843 [cs.CY]

3. Yudkowsky, E. (2019, April 15). There's no fire alarm for artificial General intelligence - Machine Intelligence Research Institute. Machine Intelligence Research Institute. https://intelligence.org/2017/10/13/fire-alarm/

4. Insider, I. (2022, August 18). False alarms make up 98% of automatic fire alarm confirmed incidents in 2020/21. IFSEC Insider | Security and Fire News and Resources. https://www.ifsecglobal.com/fire-news/false-alarms-make-up-98-of-automatic-fire-alarm-confirmed-incidents-in-2020-21/#:~:text=2023%20Fire%20Safety%20eBook%20%E2%80%93%20Grab%20your%20free%20copy!&text=Get%20your%20copy%20today!,alarm%20incidents%20are%20false%20alarms.

5. McAllester. (2014, August 12). Friendly AI and the Servant mission. Machine Thoughts. https://machinethoughts.wordpress.com/2014/08/10/friendly-ai-and-the-servant-mission/

6. Luke Muelhauser, "Eliezer Yudkowsky: Becoming a rationalist', Conversations from the Pale Blue Dot podcast, 2011 https://commonsenseatheism.com/?p=12147

7. Macey-Dare, R. (2023, June 30). How Soon is Now? Predicting the Expected Arrival Date of AGI- Artificial General Intelligence. https://papers.ssrn.com/sol3/papers.cfm?abstract_id=4496418#:~:text=This%20paper%20uses%20some%20economic,i.e.%20just%205%20years%20away

8. Edge.org. (n.d.). https://www.edge.org/response-detail/10600#:~:text=Kurzweil's%20Law%20(aka%20Law%20of,products%20of%20the%20previous%20stage.

***Why you should care***

1. Stuart Russell, Provably Benefcial Artifcial Intelligence
https://people.eecs.berkeley.edu/~russell/papers/russell-bbvabook17-pbai

2. Future of Life Institute. (2017, February 2). Provably beneficial AI | Stuart Russell [Video]. YouTube. https://www.youtube.com/watch?v=pARXQnX6QS8

3. Wang, B. (2023, April 4). AGI Expert Peter Voss Says AI Alignment Problem is Bogus | NextBigFuture.com. NextBigFuture.com. https://www.nextbigfuture.com/2023/04/agi-expert-peter-voss-says-ai-alignment-problem-is-bogus.html

## 2. The AI takeover

***What it will look like***

1. Gemini Team, Google (2024) Gemini: A Family of Highly Capable Multimodal Models
https://storage.googleapis.com/deepmind-media/gemini/gemini_1_report.pdf\

2. Vinay Pursnania, Yusuf Sermet, and Ibrahim Demir, University of Iowa, Performance of ChatGPT on the US Fundamentals of Engineering Exam: Comprehensive Assessment of Proficiency and Potential Implications for Professional Environmental Engineering Practice
arxiv:2304.12198

3. Nunes et al., Evaluating GPT-3.5 and GPT-4 Models on Brazilian University Admission Exams

4. intelligence noun - Definition, pictures, pronunciation and usage notes | Oxford Advanced Learner's Dictionary at OxfordLearnersDictionaries.com. (n.d.).
https://www.oxfordlearnersdictionaries.com/definition/english/intelligence?q=intelligence

5. David J. Chalmers, Philosophy Program, Research School of Social Sciences Australian National University. The Matrix as Metaphysics
https://consc.net/papers/matrix.pdf

6. NASA Astrobiology. (n.d.). https://astrobiology.nasa.gov/news/how-did-multicellular-life-evolve/#:~:text=The%20first%20known%20single%2Dcelled,about%20600%20million%20years%20ago

7. Proudfoot, D. (2017). *Child machines. In Oxford University Press eBooks.* https://doi.org/10.1093/oso/9780198747826.003.0040

8. Frieder, S., Pinchetti, L., Griffiths, R., Salvatori, T., Lukasiewicz, T., Petersen, P., & Berner, J. (2023, December 15). *Mathematical capabilities of ChatGPT.* https://proceedings.neurips.cc/paper_files/paper/2023/hash/58168e8a92994655d6da3939e7cc0918-Abstract-Datasets_and_Benchmarks.html

9. OpenAI, Achiam, J., Adler, S., Agarwal, S., Ahmad, L., Akkaya, I., Aleman, F. L., Almeida, D., Altenschmidt, J., Altman, S., Anadkat, S., Avila, R., Babuschkin, I., Balaji, S., Balcom, V., Baltescu, P., Bao, H., Bavarian, M., Belgum, J., . . . Zoph, B. (2023, March 15). *GPT-4 Technical Report. arXiv.org.* https://arxiv.org/abs/2303.08774

10. Shahi, R. (2023, May 9). *The universal speed of language: 39 bits per second | medium. Medium.* https://medium.com/@rohinshahi/the-universal-speed-of-language-39-bits-per-second-95cbd12ec6f7

11. Yudkowsky, E. (2008, May 23). *My childhood role model* [Online forum post]. https://www.lesswrong.com/posts/3Jpchgy53D2gB5qdk/my-childhood-role-model

**What it will look like**

1. Bostrom, N. (2016). *Superintelligence: Paths, Dangers, Strategies. Oxford University Press, USA.*

2. Mattwalsh. (2024, April 22). *ChatGPT Statistics — The key facts and figures. Style Factory.* https://www.stylefactoryproductions.com/blog/chatgpt-statistics

3. Treiber, M. (2023, July 14). *The secrets of GPT-4 leaked? IKANGAI.* https://www.ikangai.com/the-secrets-of-gpt-4-leaked/

**Yet, we will**

1. Future of Life Institute. (2024, February 21). *Pause Giant AI Experiments: An Open Letter - Future of Life Institute.* https://futureoflife.org/open-letter/pause-giant-ai-experiments/

2. Bender, E. M., Gebru, T., McMillan-Major, A., & Shmitchell, S. (2021, March). *On the Dangers of Stochastic Parrots: Can Language Models Be Too Big?.* In Proceedings of the 2021 ACM conference on fairness, accountability, and transparency (pp. 610-623).

Bostrom, N. (2016). *Superintelligence.* Oxford University Press.

Bucknall, B. S., & Dori-Hacohen, S. (2022, July). *Current and near-term AI as a potential existential risk factor.* In Proceedings of the 2022 AAAI/ACM Conference on AI, Ethics, and Society (pp. 119-129).

Carlsmith, J. (2022). *Is Power-Seeking AI an Existential Risk?.* arXiv preprint arXiv:2206.13353.

Christian, B. (2020). *The Alignment Problem: Machine Learning and human values.* Norton & Company.

Cohen, M. et al. (2022). *Advanced Artificial Agents Intervene in the Provision of Reward.* AI Magazine, 43[3] (pp. 282-293).

Eloundou, T., et al. (2023). *GPTs are GPTs: An Early Look at the Labor Market Impact Potential of Large Language Models.*

Hendrycks, D., & Mazeika, M. (2022). *X-risk Analysis for AI Research.* arXiv preprint arXiv:2206.05862.

Ngo, R. (2022). *The alignment problem from a deep learning perspective.* arXiv preprint arXiv:2209.00626.

Russell, S. (2019). *Human Compatible: Artificial Intelligence and the Problem of Control.* Viking.

Tegmark, M. (2017). *Life 3.0: Being Human in the Age of Artificial Intelligence.* Knopf.

Weidinger, L. et al (2021). *Ethical and social risks of harm from language models.* arXiv preprint arXiv:2112.04359.

Ordonez, V. et al. (2023, March 16). *OpenAI CEO Sam Altman says AI will reshape society, acknowledges risks: 'A little bit scared of this'*. ABC News.

Perrigo, B. (2023, January 12). *DeepMind CEO Demis Hassabis Urges Caution on AI*. Time.

4. Kwofie, S. K., Adams, J., Broni, E., Enninful, K. S., Agoni, C., Soliman, M. E. S., & Wilson, M. D. (2023). Artificial intelligence, machine learning, and big data for Ebola virus drug discovery. *Pharmaceuticals, 16*(3), 332. https://doi.org/10.3390/ph16030332

5. Jumper, J., Evans, R., Pritzel, A., Green, T., Figurnov, M., Ronneberger, O., Tunyasuvunakool, K., Bates, R., Žídek, A., Potapenko, A., Bridgland, A., Meyer, C., Kohl, S. a. A., Ballard, A. J., Cowie, A., Romera-Paredes, B., Nikolov, S., Jain, R., Adler, J., . . . Hassabis, D. (2021). Highly accurate protein structure prediction with AlphaFold. *Nature, 596*(7873), 583–589. https://doi.org/10.1038/s41586-021-03819-2

6. Zhang, L. (2023, September 27). *Human RideHail Crash Rate Benchmark*. Cruise. https://getcruise.com/news/blog/2023/human-ridehail-crash-rate-benchmark/?ref=warpnews.org

7. Tim Keary, Techopedia. (2024. April 9) *Top 10 Countries Leading in AI Research & Technology in 2024* https://www.techopedia.com/top-10-countries-leading-in-ai-research-technology

## 3. **The AI**

SAM

1. Wikipedia contributors. (2024, April 21). *Markov decision process*. Wikipedia. https://en.wikipedia.org/wiki/Markov_decision_process

2. Mullachery, V., Khera, A., & Husain, A. (2018, January 23). *Bayesian Neural Networks*. arXiv.org. https://arxiv.org/abs/1801.07710

3. What is a Bayesian Neural Network? (n.d.). Databricks. https://www.databricks.com/glossary/bayesian-neural-network

4. Wikipedia contributors. (2024c, June 15). *Bayesian inference*. Wikipedia. https://en.wikipedia.org/wiki/Bayesian_inference

# 4. Goals

**Instrumental convergence**

1. Instrumental convergence thesis. (n.d.). EA Forum.
https://forum.effectivealtruism.org/topics/instrumental-convergence-thesis

**Orthogonality thesis**

1. Lee, T. B. (2015, July 29). Will artificial intelligence destroy humanity? Here are 5 reasons not to worry. Vox.
https://www.vox.com/2014/8/22/6043635/5-reasons-we-shouldnt-worry-about-super-intelligent-computers-taking

2. Nick Bostrom, Future of Humanity Institute Faculty of Philosophy & Oxford Martin School Oxford University. (2012) The Superintelligent Will: Motivation And Instrumental Rationality In Advanced Artificial Agents.
https://nickbostrom.com/superintelligentwill.pdf

3. Kay, T., Keller, L., & Lehmann, L. (2020). The evolution of altruism and the serial rediscovery of the role of relatedness. Proceedings of the National Academy of Sciences of the United States of America, 117(46), 28894–28898.
https://doi.org/10.1073/pnas.2013596117

4. Schulz, W. (2022, November 9). A caveat to the Orthogonality Thesis [Online forum post].
https://www.lesswrong.com/posts/qoTpit4zFPni54GSo/a-caveat-to-the-orthogonality-thesis

5. Sharp left turn. (n.d.). AI Alignment Forum.
https://www.alignmentforum.org/tag/sharp-left-turn

6. Krakovna, V. (2022, November 29). Refining the Sharp Left Turn threat model. Victoria Krakovna.
https://vkrakovna.wordpress.com/2022/11/25/refining-the-sharp-left-turn-threat-model/#comments

## 5. Reasonability

1. *Instrumental convergence thesis. (n.d.). EA Forum.*
*https://forum.effectivealtruism.org/topics/instrumental-convergence-thesis*

### Quantilizers

1. *Jessica Taylor, Machine Intelligence Research Institute. Quantilizers: A Safer Alternative to Maximizers for Limited Optimization*
*https://intelligence.org/files/QuantilizersSaferAlternative.pdf*

### Value maximising

1. *Arora, S., & Doshi, P. (2021). A survey of inverse reinforcement learning: Challenges, methods and progress. Artificial Intelligence, 297, 103500.*
*https://doi.org/10.1016/j.artint.2021.103500*

## 6. Side effects

### Stop button problem

1. *Nate Soares and Benja Fallenstein and Eliezer Yudkowsky, Machine Intelligence Research Institute; Stuart Armstrong, Future of Humanity Institute. (2015, January 26) Corrigibility.*
*https://intelligence.org/files/Corrigibility.pdf*

### Impact regularizers

1. *Mohamed, S., & Danilo, J. R. (2015). Variational information maximisation for intrinsically motivated reinforcement learning.*
*https://proceedings.neurips.cc/paper_files/paper/2015/hash/e00406144c1e7e35240afed70f34166a-Abstract.html*

2. *Matthew E Taylor and Peter Stone. "Transfer learning for reinforcement learning domains: A survey". In: Journal of Machine Learning Research 10.Jul (2009), pp. 1633–1685*

3. *Stuart Armstrong and Benjamin Levinstein (2015). Low Impact Artificial Intelligences. arXiv preprint arXiv:1705.10720.*

# 7. Reward hacking

## Complexity

1. C. Szegedy, W. Zaremba, I. Sutskever, J. Bruna, D. Erhan, I. Goodfellow, and R. Fergus, "Intriguing properties of neural networks," arXiv preprint arXiv:1312.6199, 2013

2. Leslie Pack Kaelbling, Michael L Littman, and Anthony R Cassandra. "Planning and acting in partially observable stochastic domains". In: Artificial intelligence 101.1 (1998), pp. 99– 134.

## Metricism

1. Goodhart, C.A.E. (1984). Problems of Monetary Management: The UK Experience. In: Monetary Theory and Practice. Palgrave, London. https://doi.org/10.1007/978-1-349-17295-5_4

## Environmental embedding

1. Goodhart, C.A.E. (1984). Problems of Monetary Management: The UK Experience. In: Monetary Theory and Practice. Palgrave, London. https://doi.org/10.1007/978-1-349-17295-5_4

2. Tom Everitt and Marcus Hutter (2016, May 10). Avoiding Wireheading with Value Reinforcement Learning
arXiv preprint arXiv:1605.03143

# 8. Mesa-optimizers

## Learnt optimization

1. Evan Hubinger , Chris van Merwijk, Vladimir Mikulik , Joar Skalse, and Scott Garrabrant(2019, June 11) Risks from Learned Optimization in Advanced Machine Learning Systems
arXiv preprint arXiv:1906.01820

2. Srinivas, A., Jabri, A., Abbeel, P., Levine, S., & Finn, C. (2018, April 2). Universal Planning networks. arXiv.org. https://arxiv.org/abs/1804.00645

### Inner alignment

1. David Silver, Thomas Hubert, Julian Schrittwieser, Ioannis Antonoglou, Matthew Lai, Arthur Guez, Marc Lanctot, Laurent Sifre, Dharshan Kumaran, Thore Graepel, Timothy Lillicrap, Karen Simonyan, and Demis Hassabis. A general reinforcement learning algorithm that masters chess, shogi, and go through self-play. Science, 362(6419):1140–1144, 2018. URL https://science.sciencemag.org/content/362/ 6419/1140.full.

2. Alex Graves, Greg Wayne, and Ivo Danihelka. Neural turing machines. arXiv, 2014. URL https://arxiv.org/abs/1410.5401.

# 8. Oversight

### Adversarial oversight

1. Statista. (2023, December 19). Global surveillance technology market size 2022-2027. https://www.statista.com/statistics/1251839/surveillance-technology-market-global/

2. Stuart Armstrong, Anders Sandberg, Nick Bostrom. Thinking inside the box: using and controlling an Oracle AI https://www.aleph.se/papers/oracleAI.pdf

3. Tiku, N. (2023, May 23). The Google engineer who thinks the company's AI has come to life. Washington Post. https://www.washingtonpost.com/technology/2022/06/11/google-ai-lamda-blake-lemoine/

### Scalability

1. Wikipedia contributors. (2024d, June 16). Regulation of self-driving cars. Wikipedia. https://en.wikipedia.org/wiki/Regulation_of_self-driving_cars

2. Harris, M. (2021, June 24). Google has spent over $1.1 billion on Self-Driving tech. IEEE Spectrum. https://spectrum.ieee.org/google-has-spent-over-11-billion-on-selfdriving-techx

3.Awh, E.; Barton, B.; Vogel, E. K. (2007). Visual Working Memory Represents a Fixed Number of Items Regardless of Complexity. Psychological Science, $18^7$, 622–628. doi:10.1111/j.1467-9280.2007.01949.x

1. *Data growth worldwide 2010-2025 | Statista. (2023, November 16). Statista.*
*https://www.statista.com/statistics/871513/worldwide-data-created/*

2. *Sevilla, J. (2022, January 6). Parameter counts in Machine Learning -*
*Towards Data Science. Medium.*
*https://towardsdatascience.com/parameter-counts-in-machine-learning-*
*a312dc4753d0*

3. *Christian Daniel et al. "Active reward learning". In: Proceedings of Robotics*
*Science & Systems. 2014.*

**Absent supervisor**

1. *Leike, Jan & Martic, Miljan & Krakovna, Viktoriya & Ortega, Pedro &*
*Everitt, Tom & Lefrancq, Andrew & Orseau, Laurent & Legg, Shane. (2017). AI*
*Safety Gridworlds.*

2. *Hotten, R. (2015, December 10). Volkswagen: The scandal explained. BBC*
*News. https://www.bbc.com/news/business-34324772*

## 9. Uncertainty

**Robustness**

1. *Chen, L., Zhu, G., Li, Q., & Li, H. (2019, October 29). Adversarial example in*
*remote sensing image recognition. arXiv.org.*
*https://arxiv.org/abs/1910.13222*

**Distributional shift**

1. *Distributional shifts. (n.d.). LessWrong.*
*https://www.lesswrong.com/tag/distributional-shifts*

2. *Barnett, M. (2019, September 26). A simple environment for showing mesa*
*misalignment [Online forum post].*
*https://www.alignmentforum.org/posts/AFdRGfYDWQqmkdhFq/a-simple-*
*environment-for-showing-mesa-misalignment*

**Noise**

1. What is the uncertainty principle and why is it important? (n.d.). Caltech Science Exchange. https://scienceexchange.caltech.edu/topics/quantum-science-explained/uncertainty-principle

2. Wikipedia contributors. (2024a, March 31). Kernel method. Wikipedia. https://en.wikipedia.org/wiki/Kernel_method

3. Wikipedia contributors. (2023, August 28). Generalized method of moments. Wikipedia. https://en.wikipedia.org/wiki/Generalized_method_of_moments

4. Lars Peter Hansen. "Nobel Lecture: Uncertainty Outside and Inside Economic Models". In: Journal of Political Economy 122.5 (2014), pp. 945–987.

5. Theodore W Anderson and Herman Rubin. "The asymptotic properties of estimates of the parameters of a single equation in a complete system of stochastic equations". In: The Annals of Mathematical Statistics (1950), pp. 570–582

6. J Denis Sargan. "The estimation of relationships with autocorrelated residuals by the use of instrumental variables". In: Journal of the Royal Statistical Society. Series B (Methodological) (1959), pp. 91–105.

7. Animashree Anandkumar, Daniel Hsu, and Sham M Kakade. "A method of moments for mixture models and hidden Markov models". In: arXiv preprint arXiv:1203.0683 (2012).

# 10. Deception

**Art of lying**

1. King, B. J. (2024, February 20). Deception in the animal kingdom. Scientific American. https://www.scientificamerican.com/article/deception-in-the-animal-kingdom/

2. Greenberger, A. (2023, April 18). ARTnews.com. ARTnews.com. https://www.artnews.com/art-news/news/ai-generated-image-world-photography-organization-contest-artist-declines-award-1234664549/

3. Frankovits, G., & Mirsky, Y. (2023, June 4). Discussion paper: The threat of Real Time Deepfakes. arXiv.org. https://arxiv.org/abs/2306.02487

4. Conger, K. (2024, January 26). *Explicit Taylor Swift deepfake images elude safeguards, swamp social media.* The Seattle Times. https://www.seattletimes.com/nation-world/explicit-taylor-swift-deepfake-images-elude-safeguards-swamp-social-media/

5. Park, P. S., Goldstein, S., O'Gara, A., Chen, M., & Hendrycks, D. (2023, August 28). *AI Deception: A survey of examples, risks, and potential solutions.* arXiv.org. https://arxiv.org/abs/2308.14752

**Learnt Deception**

1. Bakhtin, A., Brown, N., Dinan, E., Farina, G., Flaherty, C., Fried, D., Goff, A., Gray, J., Hu, H., Jacob, A. P., Komeili, M., Konath, K., Kwon, M., Lerer, A., Lewis, M., Miller, A. H., Mitts, S., Renduchintala, A., Roller, S., . . . Zijlstra, M. (2022). *Human-level play in the game of Diplomacy by combining language models with strategic reasoning.* Science, 378(6624), 1067–1074. https://doi.org/10.1126/science.ade9097

2. Vinyals, O., Babuschkin, I., Czarnecki, W. M., Mathieu, M., Dudzik, A., Chung, J., Choi, D. H., Powell, R., Ewalds, T., Georgiev, P., Oh, J., Horgan, D., Kroiss, M., Danihelka, I., Huang, A., Sifre, L., Cai, T., Agapiou, J. P., Jaderberg, M., . . . Silver, D. (2019). *Grandmaster level in StarCraft II using multi-agent reinforcement learning.* Nature, 575(7782), 350–354. https://doi.org/10.1038/s41586-019-1724-z

3. Piper, K. (2019, January 25). *StarCraft is a deep, complicated war strategy game. Google's AlphaStar AI crushed it.* Vox. https://www.vox.com/future-perfect/2019/1/24/18196177/ai-artificial-intelligence-google-deepmind-starcraft-game

4. Lehman, J., Clune, J., Misevic, D., Adami, C., Altenberg, L., Beaulieu, J., Bentley, P. J., Bernard, S., Beslon, G., Bryson, D. M., Cheney, N., Chrabaszcz, P., Cully, A., Doncieux, S., Dyer, F. C., Ellefsen, K. O., Feldt, R., Fischer, S., Forrest, S., . . . Yosinski, J. (2020). *The Surprising Creativity of Digital Evolution: A Collection of Anecdotes from the Evolutionary Computation and Artificial Life Research Communities.* Artificial Life, 26(2), 274–306. https://doi.org/10.1162/artl_a_00319

5. Pock, M., Ye, A., & Moore, J. (2023, November 4). *LLMs grasp morality in concept.* arXiv.org. https://arxiv.org/abs/2311.02294

6. OpenAI (2023, March 23). *GPT-4 System Card.* https://cdn.openai.com/papers/gpt-4-system-card.pdf

7. Pan, A., Chan, J. S., Zou, A., Li, N., Basart, S., Woodside, T., Ng, J., Zhang, H., Emmons, S., & Hendrycks, D. (2023b, April 6). *Do the Rewards Justify the Means? Measuring Trade-Offs Between Rewards and Ethical Behavior in the MACHIAVELLI Benchmark*. arXiv.org. https://arxiv.org/abs/2304.03279

**Self deception**

1. Trivers, R. (2014). *Deceit and Self-Deception: Fooling Yourself the Better to Fool Others*. Penguin Books.

2. Turpin, M., Michael, J., Perez, E., & Bowman, S. R. (2023, May 7). *Language models don't always say what they think: unfaithful explanations in Chain-of-Thought prompting*. arXiv.org. https://arxiv.org/abs/2305.04388

3. Alexander, S. (2022, July 26). *ELK and the problem of truthful AI*. Astral Codex Ten. https://www.astralcodexten.com/p/elk-and-the-problem-of-truthful-ai

4. Piltch, A. (2024, May 25). *17 cringe-worthy Google AI answers demonstrate the problem with training on the entire web*. Tom's Hardware. https://www.tomshardware.com/tech-industry/artificial-intelligence/cringe-worth-google-ai-overviews

## 11. Ethics

### Pascals mugging

1. Robert_Wiblin. (2015, December 15). *Saying "AI safety research is a Pascal's Mugging" isn't a strong response* [Online forum post]. https://forum.effectivealtruism.org/posts/vYb2qEyqv76L62izD/saying-ai-safety-research-is-a-pascal-s-mugging-isn-t-a

2. *The Project Gutenberg eBook of Pascal's Pensées, by Blaise Pascal*. (n.d.). https://www.gutenberg.org/files/18269/18269-h/18269-h.htm#SECTION_III

3. Grace, K., Salvatier, J., Dafoe, A., Zhang, B., & Evans, O. (2017, May 24). *When Will AI Exceed Human Performance? Evidence from AI Experts*. arXiv.org. https://arxiv.org/abs/1705.08807

4. H.J.Otway. *Nuclear Power Plant Safety*. https://www.iaea.org/sites/default/files/publications/magazines/bulletin/bull16-1/161_202007277.pdf

**Chinese room**

1. Searle, J. R. (1980). Minds, brains, and programs. *Behavioral and Brain Sciences, 3*(3), 417–424. https://doi.org/10.1017/S0140525X00005756

**Economic Equality**

1. Innovations, patent races and endogenous growth on JSTOR. (n.d.). www.jstor.org. https://www.jstor.org/stable/41486925

2. Military technology races on JSTOR. (n.d.). www.jstor.org. https://www.jstor.org/stable/2601289

3. Pettinger, T. (2023, February 20). The Luddite Fallacy. Economics Help. https://www.economicshelp.org/blog/6717/economics/the-luddite-fallacy/

4. The National Archives. (2022, October 10). Why did the Luddites protest? - The National Archives. https://www.nationalarchives.gov.uk/education/resources/why-did-the-luddites-protest/

5. USA Capital investment, percent of GDP - data, chart | TheGlobalEconomy.com. (n.d.). TheGlobalEconomy.com. https://www.theglobaleconomy.com/usa/capital_investment/

6. USDA horse total, 1850-2012 | Data Paddock. (2019, August 11). Data Paddock. https://datapaddock.com/usda-horse-total-1850-2012/

7. Admin, F. (2021, April 29). The windfall clause: Distributing the benefits of AI - Future of Humanity Institute. The Future of Humanity Institute. https://www.fhi.ox.ac.uk/windfallclause/

8. OpenAI (2024, March 5). OpenAI and Elon Musk. https://openai.com/index/openai-elon-musk/

9. Most profitable companies worldwide 2023 | Statista. (2024, January 9). Statista. https://www.statista.com/statistics/269857/most-profitable-companies-worldwide/

**Chinese room**

1. Shead, S. (2021, March 4). U.S. is 'not prepared to defend or compete in the A.I. era,' says expert group chaired by Eric Schmidt. CNBC. https://www.cnbc.com/2021/03/02/us-not-prepared-to-defend-or-compete-in-ai-era-says-eric-schmidt-group.html? utm_source=Sailthru&utm_medium=email&utm_campaign=Recode%2010.1 3.2021&utm_term=Recode

2. Wikipedia contributors. (2024c, June 13). First strike (nuclear strategy). Wikipedia. https://en.wikipedia.org/wiki/First_strike_(nuclear_strategy)

3. Stevenson, P. W. (2021, November 25). 10 of Antonin Scalia's quirkiest and most scathing quotes. Washington Post. https://www.washingtonpost.com/news/the-fix/wp/2016/02/13/10-of-antonin-scalias-quirkiest-and-most-scathing-quotes/

4. The most expensive election ever. (n.d.). Brennan Center for Justice. https://www.brennancenter.org/our-work/analysis-opinion/most-expensive-election-ever

5. Giattino, C., Mathieu, E., Samborska, V., & Roser, M. (2024, January 31). Artificial intelligence. Our World in Data. https://ourworldindata.org/artificial-intelligence

6. Personalized Online Advertising Effectiveness: the interplay of what, when, and where on JSTOR. (n.d.). www.jstor.org. https://www.jstor.org/stable/24544741

7. Burtell, M., & Woodside, T. (2023, March 15). Artificial Influence: An Analysis of AI-Driven Persuasion. arXiv.org. https://arxiv.org/abs/2303.08721

8. Kleinberg, S., & Marsh, J. K. (2023). Less is more: information needs, information wants, and what makes causal models useful. Cognitive Research, 8(1). https://doi.org/10.1186/s41235-023-00509-7

9. Archives. (2019, August 18). Too much information: ineffective intelligence collection. Harvard International Review. https://hir.harvard.edu/too-much-information/

10. Brañas-Garza, P., Bucheli, M., & Espinosa, M. P. (2020). *Altruism and information. Journal of Economic Psychology, 81, 102332.* https://doi.org/10.1016/j.joep.2020.102332

11. Thomson, J. (2024, January 26). *People who don't understand pregnancy more likely to oppose abortion. Newsweek.* https://www.newsweek.com/abortion-rights-supported-people-who-understand-pregnancy-1863873

12. VHEMT. (n.d.). https://www.vhemt.org/

### Resources for change

1. *AI Regulation is Coming- What is the Likely Outcome? (n.d.).* https://www.csis.org/blogs/strategic-technologies-blog/ai-regulation-coming-what-likely-outcome

2. *Understanding the UN report on ozone layer recovery. (2023, January 31). The Hub.* https://hub.jhu.edu/2023/01/31/un-report-ozone-layer-recovery/

3. *Change in the consumption of ozone-depleting substances. (n.d.). Our World in Data.* https://ourworldindata.org/grapher/ozone-depleting-substances-index

4. Yudkowsky, E. (2023, March 29). *Pausing AI Developments Isn't Enough. We Need to Shut it All Down. TIME.* https://time.com/6266923/ai-eliezer-yudkowsky-open-letter-not-enough/

5. *Statement on AI Risk | CAIS. (n.d.).* https://www.safe.ai/work/statement-on-ai-risk

6. *MATS program. (n.d.). ML Alignment & Theory Scholars.* https://www.matsprogram.org/

7. *AI Safety Camp. (n.d.).* https://aisafety.camp/

www.ingramcontent.com/pod-product-compliance
Lightning Source LLC
LaVergne TN
LVHW051442050326
832903LV00030BD/3193